The Battle-F
Allan Corstorphin Smith

including

Deadly Art of Judo

and

10 Ways to "Get" a Boche

The Battle-Fighting Combatives of Allan Corstorphin Smith

including

Deadly Art of Judo

and

10 Ways to "Get" a Boche

Compiled and edited by

Robert H. Sabet

Lost Arts Publications

THE BATTLE-FIGHTING COMBATIVES OF ALLAN C. SMITH
Copyright © 2020 Robert H. Sabet

All rights reserved. This book or any portion thereof may not be reproduced or used in any manner whatsoever without the express written permission of the publisher except for the use of brief quotations in a book review or scholarly journal.

This publication may contain copyrighted material the use of which was not authorized by the copyright owner. Such material is made available in an effort to advance understanding of the topic discussed in the publication. This constitutes fair use of any such copyrighted material as provided for in section 107 of the US Copyright Law. If you wish to use copyrighted material from this site for purposes of your own that go beyond fair use, you must obtain permission from the copyright owner. If you are the copyright owner and would like this content removed from this title, please contact us via the publisher.

ISBN: 978-1-716-34511-1

First Printing: October 2020

Lost Arts Publications
Brooklyn, NY 11235

LOST ARTS PUBLICATIONS

The Battle-Fighting Combatives of Allan Corstorphin Smith

CONTENTS

Dedication 7

Foreword 9

Introduction 11

Book I
Deadly Art of Judo

Becoming A Black Belt 17

Setting Sail on the Tenyu Maru 23

Stahara 27

Six Deadly Lessons from A Black Belt Master 33

Camp Upton, Long Island 49

Kogiro Haneishi 55

Benny Leonard 63

Book II
10 Ways to "Get" a Boche

Introduction 75

First Way: *Seized Round Waist From Front* (1) 85

Second Way: *Seized Round Waist From Front* (2) 87

Third Way: *Attacked With Chin Hold* 89

Fourth Way: *Attacked From Behind* (1) 93

Fifth Way: *Attacked From Behind* (2) 95

Sixth Way: *Attempted Throttle* 99
Seventh Way: *The Wrist Breaking Twist* 103
Eighth Way: *The Elbow Break* 107
Ninth Way: *Stalking a Sentry Noiselessly* 111
Tenth Way: *Jiu-jitsu and the Bayonet* 115
Instructor to New York State Troopers 119
Safety Monitors at the World's Fair 129
Working for the Red Cross 135
Battle-Fighting 141
End Comments 147

About the Editor 149
Bibliography 151

DEDICATION

This book is dedicated to my wife Angela and my daughter Katelyn. They helped me to *Keep Calm And Carry On* during the Covid lockdown when I was finally able to sort through my research and put my thoughts to paper.

Thanks also to Coach Jose Toledo from Untouchables Sullivan County Boxing Club for keeping me fighting fit these many months.

Thank you James Loriega, Fernan Vargas, and Twin Ravens for accepting what I wrote and for helping to make it accessible.

Thank you Matt Temkin for taking the time to demonstrate and train me in WW II-Era hand-to-hand Combat Techniques, when I was just starting out on the journey to really understand what it was all about.

Thank you Chris Hennessey of *Dynamic Fighting Concepts*, for being my Instructor and training partner and for helping me to further my understanding of hand-to-hand Fighting, and defensive tactics.

Thanks to Jean Marc, the head of *Federation Internationale de Close Combat* for his support.

Also a big thank you to Phil Matthews, Dave Kentner, Steve Brown, Francis Patrick and the members of Rough And Tumble Society for their help, their encouragement and their words of advice.

About the Publisher

Lost Arts Publications was established in 2015 to satisfy the growing interest in unique, rare, and almost-lost martial disciplines, arts, and systems. Niche-focused on lesser-known and rarely-seen methods, from both Eastern and Western perspectives, Lost Arts Publications produces original works in both hardcover and paperback formats.

Two imprints also publish under the Lost Arts Publications banner. The *Pay-Per-Cut Press* imprint specializes in edged weapons and systems of European origin. The *Raven Tradecraft Press* imprint specializes in modern spycraft and civilian tradecraft.

Foreword

A researcher's interests are more than a hobby, if done badly it shows—if done well this also shows. The truth has a habit of being found out, it doesn't stop people passing out half baked "facts" or outright falsehoods though. True research is certainly not for the faint of heart, easily offended or for those who desire easily obtained gratifications. I wonder about the motivations of those with the latter, are they sincere? Do they really want to share knowledge and the history of those who gave so much in our past? Or do they have their own agendas they are keeping to themselves?

True research is about time and work, not only in seeking out source materials, books, annotations, people of interest and getting access to (and spending more time in) dusty archives. It's not only about constantly sorting the wheat from the chaff but also sometimes sorting the truth from the lie. It is hard work.

It's about being continually reflective, unbiased and focused – more time spent, more hard work.

You spend a lot of time arranging things as well as actually obtaining the research materials. You spend a lot of time conversing with people, making connections. Sometimes they are helpful, they might not have the same particular interest but know of something or somewhere that they have come across that might help you in your quest. They share this with you, they give you faith in the human race.

From my own personal experience, it's the ones who claim the same interests that you have to be careful of, as W.E Fairbairn once said "Don't let anyone lead you down the garden path". It makes you wonder what the Human race has come to at times. You have to be continually reflective and never take anything at another's word. Your independent research must show the same findings or you will continue to perpetuate another's fallacy or propaganda.

I have researched Combatives for nearly thirty years and from that I can say honestly that it has made me a very good judge of people. I have encountered some of the great and some of the worst, you learn quickly who you can trust.

I can honestly and whole-heartedly recommend Robert Sabet and his research. I trust both his research and his work ethic toward it. He is sincere and reflective; he does his own research.

With this and future works he is looking further than any of us previously went before, going to the places that were just as (or if not more important) than the well-worn rehashed topics.

He has my trust.

Moreover—he made a jaded researcher enjoy his hobbies again. I am personally very much looking forward to his future research works!

—Phil Matthews
thebristolbloke@gmail.com
15 oct 2020

Introduction

I first became aware of Allan Corstorphin Smith many years ago while searching through an archive of hand-to-hand combat manuals which someone had graciously posted to an internet forum. Smith's series of manuals titled **The Secrets of Jiu-Jitsu** had been put on-line in order to share the knowledge they contained with someone such as myself who was searching for that same knowledge.

At the time I stumbled upon the archive I was focused on finding the works of the pioneers of Combatives. I was seeking any and all information I could find on such notable personalities as William E. Fairbairn, Rex Applegate, Anthony Joseph Drexel Biddle Sr. as well as other lesser-known individuals, such as Francois D'Eliscu and Stephen Stavers.

While Smith's works were interesting, my focus was elsewhere with the more-renown ones. At the time I was not aware that he, too, taught the troops during the Second World War, so I put his stuff off to the side. I liked what I saw in the World War Two-era manuals and wanted to know more about the no-nonsense, dirty fighting systems that men like Fairbairn and Applegate had pioneered. Soon I sought out instructors who could give me their take on it.

Of course, by the time I decided to seek out training on the subject, most of the Veterans of that conflict were beyond any sort of teaching ability. It was now their children that I would seek out to learn from, if they were willing to pass anything on. Although I had an uncle who was in the Marines and showed me a few Judo moves, I was quite young at the time and did not fully appreciate the lessons. I was now at a point where I wanted to know more.

There were various reasons for my seeking out this type of training, one of the main ones being that I was no longer interested in learning traditional martial arts. I wanted something more direct and bare bones; something that didn't take years to learn but was highly effective and battle-tested.

Years later I became aware of a training video from 1917, filmed at Camp Benning, in which Allan Smith is portrayed teaching some Jiu-Jitsu moves. However, once again, for me it was the wrong era and so I had blinders on. I had still been focused on finding anything World War Two related when it came to unarmed combat training or "Judo" as they liked to call it back then. It was not the Judo of the Japanese but an Americanized form of Rough and Tumble fighting that included elements of Judo, but also incorporated elements of Savate and Boxing and other fighting systems.

Several more years went by and as I started digging deeper, it became clearer to me via the research of others that World War One had an influence on the Combatives of the Second World War. Surely, the Veterans of that conflict had been called upon to pass on any knowledge they had gained. Much in the same way that fathers took their sons who were about to be shipped off to Vietnam and showed them a thing or two which they had picked up in the Second World War.

The thing I realized was that for every Fairbairn or Biddle there was a corresponding Robert Seeger out of Camp Haan or Arvin Ghazlo out of Camp Lejeune who taught countless troops how to save their bacon if they got caught in a situation where they no longer had the use of their weapon.

Allan Smith was one of the people who passed on what he knew. He was definitely one of the unsung Combatives pioneers of the era. Essentially Allan Smith stripped down the Jiu-Jitsu he had learned at the Kodokan and taught something in World War One which was very similar to what the other Combatives pioneers taught later on. In World War Two he called his system **Battle Fighting**.

During the course of my research I found newspaper articles Smith had written in 1917 which further helped me to understand the man and his system. Later I was able to locate one of his unpublished works which he had written in 1918 in order to help teach the troops his system. I have transcribed the articles and the pamphlet and included them with my research here.

I used the article *Some Background on Captain Allan Corstorphin Smith, Author of Secrets of Jiu-Jitsu: A Complete Course in Self Defense (1920)*, written by Richard Bowen for the Journal of Non-lethal Combatives, June 2003 for some of the background on Smith's early years of training at Kodokan. I attempted to reach out to the Kodokan to see if I could find the article mentioned. I realized that I did not have a lot about Smith in his youth other than what was mentioned in Bowen's article. I also have been unable to find anything further on Smith past 1946. Hopefully what I have provided here was enough to bring some recognition to the man for his efforts during both conflicts.

I feel I have a kinship with Smith as he was from Scotland as were some of my relatives who lived in New York during the same time period that he immigrated to the United States. He settled in Queens later in life not far from where I live today, and my Grandfather attended the World's Fair, where Smith instructed the safety monitors. I really appreciate that Smith was from another country, traveled overseas to pursue a goal, then came here and sought to help people from so many different walks of life. He gave them the tools to feel safer and more secure about themselves in their lives whomever they were, whether they were a student, a boy scout, a policeman or a soldier.

—Robert H. Sabet
New York, 2020

The Battle-Fighting Combatives of Allan Corstorphin Smith
Book I

Becoming a Black Belt

Allan Corstorphin Smith, was born on the 4th of February 1884 in Newcastleton, Scotland. He was the product of his father's second marriage. Newcastleton is a village in the Scottish Borders, a few miles from the border with England, on the Liddel Water.

According to one article Allan Smith got into the military physical training game in his youth because he was beaten up by a town bully. As most youths do when they were bullied, Smith took up boxing as a form of self-protection.

Eventually he got pretty good at the manly art of self-defense and one night in Glasgow at a theater he decided to accept an offer to meet all comers made by a Japanese Jiu-Jitsu expert. Although Smith was unable to defeat him, he was impressed by the ability of the smaller man to deal with a much larger opponent and this began his lifelong interest in learning Jiu-Jitsu. This led him to ask his parents to send him to Japan.

In the beginning Smith was unable to travel to the Kodokan Judo Institute in Tokyo for lessons as much as he wanted, so instead he built his own dojo and invited others to attend. One of his training partners, a Japanese man named Sato was a 3rd Dan. Occasionally other Japanese would train with Smith at his dojo. One of the most notable was Kyuzo Mifune who was 5th Dan.

U. S. DEPARTMENT OF LABOR
NATURALIZATION SERVICE

No. 20-M

ORIGINAL

UNITED STATES OF AMERICA

PETITION FOR NATURALIZATION

To the Honorable the SUPREME COURT OF THE DISTRICT OF COLUMBIA at WASHINGTON, D. C.

The petition of **Allan Corstorphin Smith** respectfully shows:

First. My place of residence is WASHINGTON, D. C.

Second. My occupation is **SOLDIER; Special Detail to Commission on Training Camp Activities**

Third. I was born on the **4th** day of **February**, anno Domini 1 **884**, at **Newcastleton, Scotland**

Fourth. I emigrated to the United States from _____ on or about the _____

anno Domini 1____, and arrived in the United States, at the port of _____ on the _____ day of _____ anno Domini 1____, on the vessel _____

Fifth. I declared my intention to become a citizen of the United States on the _____ day of _____ Court at _____ anno Domini 1____.

Sixth. I am **not** married.

Petition filed under provision of act of May 9th, 1918.
I entered the U.S. Army on **June 12**, 1918 and am still in the service.

Seventh. I am not a disbeliever in or opposed to organized government... particularly **George V, King of Great Britain & Ireland** of whom at this time I am a subject, and it is my intention to reside permanently in the United States.

Eighth. I am able to speak the English language.

Ninth. I have resided continuously in the United States... since the **6th** day of **September**, anno Domini 1 **917**...

Tenth. I have not heretofore made petition for citizenship to any court.

Allan Corstorphin Smith
(Complete and true signature of petitioner.)

AFFIDAVITS OF PETITIONER AND WITNESSES

United States of America
District of Columbia } ss:

Allan Corstorphin Smith

Julian LaR. Harris occupation SOLDIER, 1st Lieut. USNA residing at WASHINGTON, D. C.
and **Humphrey T. Nichols** occupation SOLDIER, 1st Lieut. U.S.A. residing at WASHINGTON, D. C.

Allan Corstorphin Smith ... since the **6th** day of **October** anno Domini 1 **917**...

Julian LaRose Harris
(Signature of witness.)
Humphrey T. Nichols
(Signature of witness.)

Subscribed and sworn to before me... this **17th** day of **June**, anno Domini 1918.

_____, Clerk.
By _____, Deputy Clerk.

[OVER]

A fluent speaker of Japanese, German, and French, Smith managed to publish a book in Yokohama in 1915 titled **Little Lessons in Japanese**. He would later go on to author several other books the most notable of them being, **The Secrets of Jiu-Jitsu**. He also wrote **The Spartan Law** and **Safety in the World of Tomorrow**.

In 1916 after nine years of training to reach the required proficiency, the last three of which were in earnest, Smith received his Shodan "beginning degree" the lowest black belt rank at the Kodokan. As noted, up until that time only a handful of foreigners had the right to wear the coveted decoration, hundreds had tried and failed after long sessions of training and competition.

One foreigner who succeeded was E.J. Harrison who formerly edited the American paper in Japan and became the war correspondent at Petrograd. Harrison later went on to write the classic book, **Fighting Spirit of Japan**, in 1913.

Another man, David T. Weed, was a professor of languages who was of mixed Japanese American ancestry, his mother was Japanese. There was W.E. Steers a Londoner who got his black belt in 1912 and was first secretary at the Budokwai and along with Harrison contributed to making Kano's Judo better known to British readers through his writings. Finally, there was V.S. Oshchepkov, a Russian who got his rank in 1913 and who later pioneered Judo and Sambo in the Soviet Union.

From the time a man entered the Judo school a complete record was kept of all the student's matches, showing which opponents he had met and with what result, and what tricks had won him the match. There were hundreds of tricks each with its own name. Smith said that for every catch in catch-as-catch can, or Greco-Roman wrestling, there are ten in Jiu-Jitsu.

He went on the make the claim that between the Japanese art of self-defense and Western wrestling there was no comparison. He included boxing in the list of arts which he considered to be inferior to Jiu-Jitsu.

In one interview Smith said that—

"Among Americans and Europeans, an idea prevails that jiu-jitsu is simply a lot of holds that would be debarred in a western wrestling match, and is consequently inferior to the catch-as-catch can style. This is all wrong. This idea might be applicable to the old Jiu-Jitsu but the modern cult is simply a very scientific form of wrestling, including a number of throws with which our less scientific catch-as-catch-can wrestlers are not acquainted."

Smith claimed that *"A master of Jiu-Jitsu could have defeated Jack Johnson in his prime. My friend here,"* indicating his instructor, *"would have had no trouble in defeating Johnson."*

"Or Jess Willard?" a visitor asked. Smith did not reply but his teacher said he was confident that at least thirty of his pupils could beat either Willard or Johnson.

Smith expressed pride in being a Scot in an interview in the March 1916 issue of the Kodokan magazine, **Judo**. Smith said that the Scots took pride in their traditions in the same way that the Japanese took pride in their own traditions.

In the article he discussed the Scottish victory over the English at Bannockburn in 1314. He added that Germany was exaggerating the enmity between the Scots and the English, saying "*We are all British now*." The statement was made during the First World War when Japan and Britain were allies during that conflict.

Smith eventually tried to enlist in the British Army at the British consulate in Yokohama but was rejected after a medical examination. The medical staff determined that Smith was unfit for service because of bronchitis.

By chance during a demonstration before military attaches in Tokyo, he was encouraged to go to the United States to teach Judo to the troops. He resigned from his job at the American Trading Company and decided to set sail for the States.

U. S. DEPARTMENT OF LABOR
NATURALIZATION SERVICE
ORIGINAL 95

No. 68186

UNITED STATES OF AMERICA

DECLARATION OF INTENTION

☞ Invalid for all purposes seven years after the date hereof

State of New York, } ss: In the District Court of the United States.
Southern District of New York,

I, Allan Corstorphin Smith, aged 33 years, occupation Instructor, do declare on oath that my personal description is: Color white, complexion fair, height 5 feet 4 inches, weight 135 pounds, color of hair brown, color of eyes blue, other visible distinctive marks none. I was born in Roxboroughshire, Scotland, on the 4 day of May, anno Domini 1884, now reside at 123 East 30 St. (Give number and street.), New York City, N. Y. I emigrated to the United States of America from Yokohama, Japan, on the vessel Tenyo Maru (If the alien arrived otherwise than by vessel, the character of conveyance or name of transportation company should be given.); my last foreign residence was Japan; I am not married; the name of my wife is _____; she was born at _____ and now resides at _____. It is my bona fide intention to renounce forever all allegiance and fidelity to any foreign prince, potentate, state, or sovereignty, and particularly to George V, King of Great Britain and Ireland, of whom I am now a subject; I arrived at the port of San Francisco, in the State of California, on or about the 6 day of Sept, anno Domini 1917; I am not an anarchist; I am not a polygamist nor a believer in the practice of polygamy; and it is my intention in good faith to become a citizen of the United States of America and to permanently reside therein: SO HELP ME GOD.

Allan Corstorphin Smith
(Original signature of declarant.)

Subscribed and sworn to before me in the office of the Clerk of said Court at New York City, N. Y., this 2 day of Feby anno Domini 1918.

[SEAL.]

ALEX GILCHRIST, JR.,
Clerk of the District Court of the United States.

By _____, Deputy Clerk.

SETTING SAIL ON THE TENYO MARU

On August 22nd, 1917 an article in the **Japanese Times** states that Smith was one of the passengers on the Tenyo Maru which left Yokohama for San Francisco. Smith was on his way to the States along with a Japanese Judoist. It's unclear who the Judoist was but a later article in the Brooklyn Times Union, Tuesday, March, 5th 1918 states that a man named "Haneishi, the wiry and skillful Jap, who assists Mr. Smith at Upton, is said to be one of the fastest men on his feet in Japan."

Smith writes in **The Secrets of Jiu-Jitsu,** "Mr. Haneishi, the Jiujitsu expert I brought from Japan with me, besides being a professional teacher of the art is also a bone-setter, and general first-aid practitioner."

It was Smith's goal to offer his services to the Government in Washington as a Judo expert. In his petition for naturalization in 1918, Smith states that his occupation is Soldier; Special Detail to Commission on Training Camp Activities.

Having become a citizen and commissioned a Captain, Smith was made an instructor in Jiu-Jitsu and was sent to various cantonments throughout the country. During the conflict he instructed more than 100,000 men and 20,000 officers in that method of self-defense.

It was also during this time period that he did a series of six newspaper articles describing some of the techniques he thought were useful for the citizen and soldier in a situation where they might be required to defend themselves in hand-to-hand fighting.

These lessons were titled **Deadly Art Of Judo**, *Lessons, By A Black Belt Master.*

Later in 1918 while stationed at Camp Upton he would write a pamphlet titled **10 Ways To "Get" A Boche,** in which he demonstrates ten different hand-to-hand combat techniques that could be used to protect allied soldiers in trench warfare.

In 1920 Smith published a work in seven volumes which has been reprinted and is widely available today. The title of those volumes was **The Secrets of Jiu-jitsu:** *A Complete Course in Self Defense.*

Later in his life, Allan Smith was residing in Jackson Heights, Queens and had been working as the Director of the Red Cross. He had achieved the rank of Major and was affiliated with the New York Military Training Commission as State director of physical training where he had charge of physical and military training of 300,000 cadets. He was then appointed the commandant of the Knickerbocker Greys, the 7th Regiment Cadet Corps.

Smith had later been appointed physical training officer for the 27th Division under General John F. O'Ryan and subsequently accepted the position of military instructor for the New York State Police. In addition, Smith had also been chosen as military instructor to the New York World's Fair uniformed personnel, where he also gave special training to more that 6,000 Boy Scouts.

THE BATTLE FIGHTING COMBATIVES OF ALLAN C. SMITH

STAHARA

There is a frequent reference made in both **10 Ways To "Get" A Boche** as well as **The Secrets of Jiu-Jitsu** regarding the shita hara or lower abdomen, which Smith abbreviated as, "Stahara."

Smith described how the word "Stahara" originated in **The Secrets of Jiu-Jitsu**—

> When I commenced to teach Jiu-jitsu in Yokohama, Japan, in every trick I showed how to use the lower abdomen, and how to maneuver the opponent's balance. My first pupils were Japanese friends, and lower abdomen to them was *shita hara*.
>
> Shita (pronounced sh'ta) and hara are two Japanese words meaning under or lower abdomen. The words shita hara mean to a Japanese what the words lower abdomen mean to us - and nothing more.
>
> This word *hara* is the same word we meet in *hara kiri*—abdomen cutting—the Japanese method of suicide. Gradually as I evolved the idea of balance-control and abdominal power, I adopted the word *shita-hara* as a technical term for a new principle for which there was no name.

Newspaper Article illustrating the location of the Stahara by Robert L. Ripley, in the *Saskatoon Daily Star*, Thursday, December 19th, 1918. Note: Benny Leonard Uses It.

When teaching the Doughboys, they called it "Stahara" and that is how it was finally written. It is an American word for an American idea.

STA-HA-RA sta—pronounced as in star.
ha—pronounced as in harp.
ra—a has the same sound as in the first two syllables.

Smith goes on to explain that Japanese teachers of Jiu-jitsu do not mention the Stahara when explaining a throw or trick to their disciples. They teach the use of the arms and legs, of the hips and shoulders, but do not show the principle of balance which is the basis of the whole system.

It is therefore an average of ten years before a student of Jiu-jitsu in Japan masters these throws. It takes that length of time to acquire the scientific way, in common parlance, to "get the knack" of doing the trick.

Jiu-jitsu is not done with strength of arm or leg and this inability to grasp the underlying principle is why it takes so long to master it.

You must realize the importance of the Stahara. It is here the center of gravity lies. It is here the seat of the emotions lies. It is the most important part of the human body, and the most neglected.

In 1918 Robert L. Ripley got wind of what Stahara was all about and wrote an article, in which he *Contrasts Jap and American Training Plans.*

He writes—
"Stahara is a Japanese secret. It means—*sta* lower; *hara*, abdomen—lower abdomen.

"The Japanese pay all attention to the development of the Stahara or stomach muscles because in the Stahara lies the secret of their remarkable athletic effectiveness—particularly in Jiu-Jitsu.

"They place here the seat of courage and the centre of equilibrium, drawing the conclusion that a studied muscular development of this region gives more courage to the already brave and stability to the strong.

"You may test the value of the Stahara by first assuming the white man's attitude of defiance—chin up, head back, chest thrown out, one foot planted in front of the other. A slight push will put you off balance—particularly if you are shoved sideways."

He continues,
"Then try the Japanese way—contract your Stahara—just tighten your belt in other words. Allow someone to push you and you will find yourself as firm as a rock.

"The Jap never throws his chest out nor tilts his chin up when danger threatens as the white man has been wont to do for centuries. The wily Jap knows that our popular heroic attitude is the weakest of all defensive or offensive postures.

"The Jap merely spreads his feet slightly and contracts his stomach muscles—the Stahara, and he is ready for anything.

"The Stahara is invaluable in all branches of athletics —particularly boxing and wrestling.

"A side view of a skeleton will give an idea of the bony structure of the body. The thorax and pelvis are joined by the column of lumbar vertebrae. This column is flexible and has to depend on the strength of the surrounding muscles for its rigidity. A glance will show you the part the muscles of the Stahara play and why the Japanese lay such importance on their development. A development of the Stahara leads to a better union of the limbs—that is, the arms are more strongly connected with the legs.

"The Japanese athlete in crouching lowers the centre of equilibrium and a strong Stahara keeps it lowered. In other words, they have applied the principle of loaded dice to the human body. The centre of equilibrium has "been made non-coincident with the centre of the body, and the light side stays more easily uppermost.

"As for the courage part—with preparedness comes courage. Development and contraction of the muscles of the Stahara give the body its maximum stability and with this comes the assurance of being capable of greater resistance."

JUJUTSU FOR OUR SOLDIERS.

One of the most expert instructors in the art of jujutsu, Mr. Allan Smith, sailed from Yokohama on Aug. 21 and will proceed to the various military training camps in the United States, where, during the coming winter, he will lecture on and teach jujutsu. He claims that in a course of six lessons he can indicate the mysteries of the Japanese mode of self-defense and can show to whole regiments at a time tricks of agility that will enable soldiers to disable an opponent in a hand-to-hand fight—where they are too close for weapons. In capturing trenches, he insists, a knowledge of jujutsu is invaluable and will prove a veritable life-saver.

Mr. Smith's ability has been proved by an award to him of "the black belt," the athletic trophy for proficiency in the art. A long time is necessary to completely master jujutsu.—East and West News.

Dayton Daily News, Tuesday October 2nd, 1917

SIX DEADLY LESSONS
BY A BLACK BELT MASTER

Lesson 1.

To make American soldiers or others Judo experts in a short time will of course be impossible.

To give them a knowledge of the fundamentals of Judo and instruct them in the grips, kicks and blows necessary in emergencies will not be difficult.

In my first article it may be well to refer to the origin of Judo and its effect upon the morale of the Japanese people. Judo (Jiu-Jitsu as it is more commonly known in the U.S.) may be traced back hundreds of years in Japan.

Always adepts at the arts of fencing and archery, the Japanese discovered that often they could discard their own weapon, step inside an opponent's guard and kill him with a blow or kick upon a vital spot.

Soon they began practicing these blows as a thing apart from actual fencing. In the course of time Judo was evolved.

Before Port Arthur there were many hand-to-hand struggles in which Japanese almost invariably won out. Every man in the Japanese army and navy is taught the art of self-defense and attack without use of arms. These men are not as a rule, Judo experts. But they do possess knowledge of the kicks, grips, and, if necessary, death-dealing blows against the ordinary rough opponent.

The Japanese government insists upon this training, not so much with a view to securing practical results in an actual fight but because of the increased military morale that comes from confidence in physical prowess.

Knowledge that he probably is more than able to cope hand-to-hand with an opponent has caused the Japanese soldier to become known as a "human bullet" though he may be fighting at a distance.

To be a real Judo man requires years of study, practice and stern competition. Most officers are Judo men. As a rule the great Japanese statesman is a Judo graduate and practitioner of Judo ethics.

In coming to the United States I hope to see Judo (Jiu-Jitsu) introduced into schools and colleges; first on account of its value as a means of self-defense; secondly because of the physical training and even more so for the self-restraint and sense of discipline it inspires.

My immediate hope is to teach the soldiers what to do in "close up" fighting especially when all other weapons have vanished but the body itself.

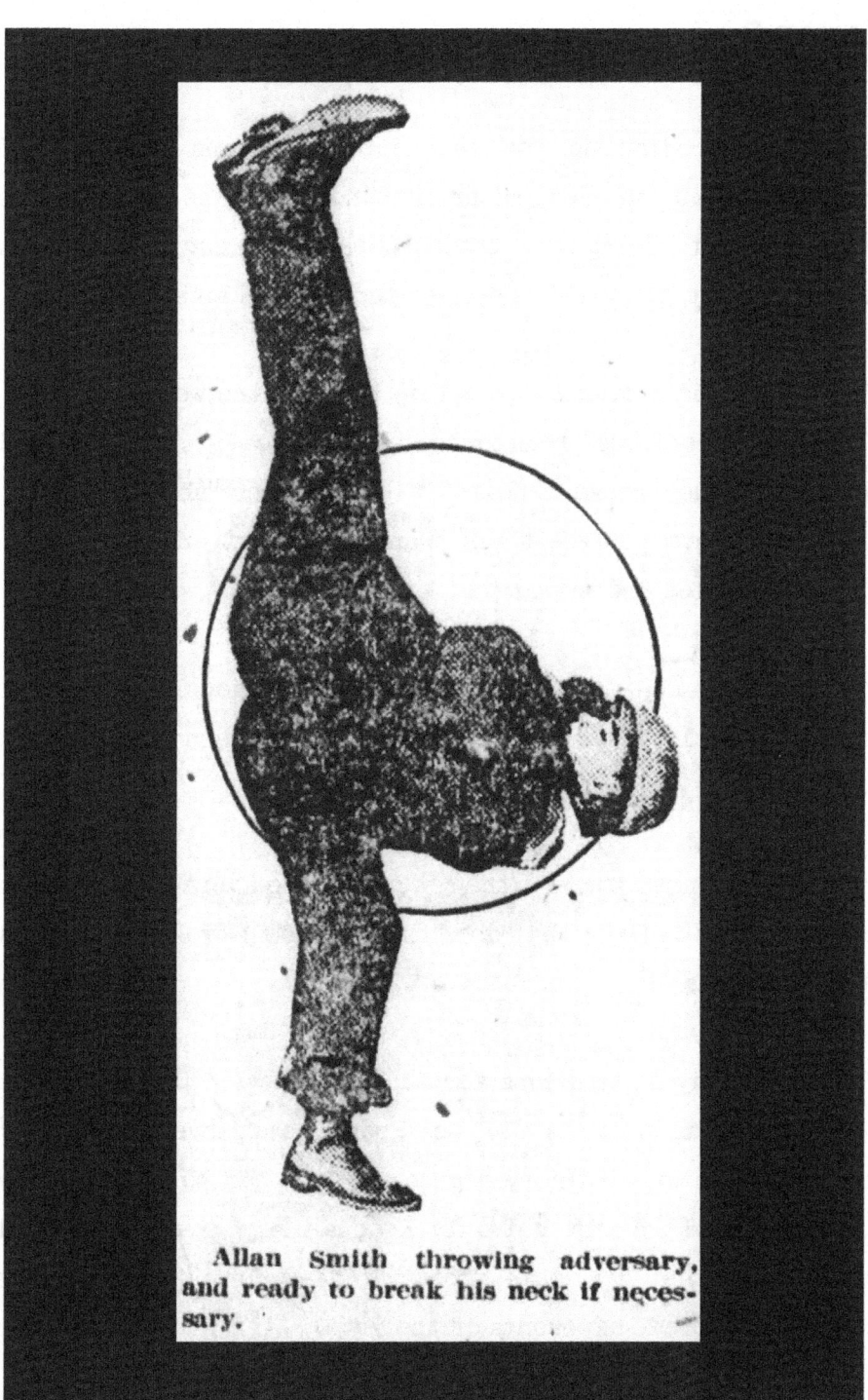

Allan Smith throwing adversary, and ready to break his neck if necessary.

Lesson 2.

Judo, or Jiu-Jitsu as you call it here, means "the art of yielding." But do not misunderstand. Judo is merely the appearance of giving way before superior strength when as a matter of fact, the yield is a trick to vanquish an assailant.

You have noticed tree limbs fallen beneath the weight of snow. These trees offered resistance to the heavy snowfall and inevitably they broke beneath it. Other trees "shed" the snow. After the storm you see their branches unhurt and erect. They had not resisted the snow.

Trained Judo men take falls that would seriously injure the strongest athlete not used to the method of non-resistance in falling.

It is the extended arm and the set jaw of the average person who realizes he is falling that does the damage in broken bones and torn ligaments.

There are many institutions for Judo instruction in Japan, from the provincial schools up to Kodokan college, the great governing center. Ordinary degrees in Judo can be conferred by the provincial schools, but only Kodokan may give the coveted black belt, the legitimate possessor of which is regarded as among the supreme exponents of the art.

Thousands of students are graded in different classes on up to highest. A student is rated by his success in defeating the mediocre, then the best men of any class. When he has proved himself superior to any in a given class he is sent to the higher ones until his limit is reached.

A student is never sent up as a result of one match. He must prove himself in many matches. It is not possible here to touch upon innumerable phases of the training given the young man in Japan, but the national and racial independence so noticeable in the individual Japanese is largely due to confidence in his physical fitness.

Smith, at right, foiling armed assailant.

Lesson 3.

In the previous article we referred to the appearance of yielding as essential in successful Judo. We stipulated that the apparent yielding was simply a trick to outwit an assailant - to use his strength in defeating his own purposes.

To illustrate the yielding idea:
A big, heavy man, intent on mischief has placed a hand on each of your shoulders and is pushing you backward.

Seize the moment when he gives you a vicious shove on one shoulder or the other. Say, for instance, he has given you a hard shove with his right arm.

Grasp him by his right sleeve with your left hand, give him an equally vicious pull in the same direction.

You step sidewise to your right thus evading the force of his right shoulder.

At the same time, with your left foot you prevent his stepping forward with is right leg. This causes him to lose his balance and hurls him to the ground.

Note that during all this time the assaulted person has not had to exert himself greatly.

If you happen to give a man a pull in exactly the right direction and trip him properly he is liable to be hurt. So be careful while practicing until you and your companion learn how to fall properly.

Lesson 4.

A large man or very strong opponent may come at you with the intention of seizing you firmly around the waist and bearing you to the ground. Judo has a remedy for this fellow.

As he comes, do not allow him to secure a firm hold on you. Here is the way to prevent it:

Step quickly in to meet him, placing the palm of one hand beneath his chin, the other hand around the small of his back. Pull him toward you with the arm behind his back, pushing his head backward with the other hand.

If necessary the assailant can be thrown to the ground in this way, which would be a correct method in case of self-defense against an attack by a man who was intent on injury.

In practicing with a friend stop short of throwing him to the ground and take care not to jerk his head back too quickly or severe injury might result to the back of his neck. If one is careful both parties trying to learn this trick may derive considerable pleasure and finally become adepts.

Lesson 5.

In our preceding article we described the counter when a man tries to seize you around the waist. This counter was in placing one hand under his chin, forcing his head back and using the other hand around his back.

But sometimes a man succeeds in pinning one or both of your arms to your side, as in photo No. 1. Judo has a prescription for this predicament. Already your arms have been pinned. The photos here show the Judo scientific Cross Buttock as it is operated.

Grasp the right sleeve of your opponent with your left hand as in photo No. 2. Press his left shoulder close to your chest. At the same time your right hand slips around his waist.

You turn inward toward your right, throwing your back in front of his body. Your left foot is in front of his left foot and your right before his right as in illustration. Do not bend forward.

By bending the knees sidewise, lower your body about six inches. Strike the front of his right thigh with your buttock, bending forward at the same time. By the hold on his right sleeve with your left hand and your right arm across his back get him in position as shown in photo No. 3.

From this position it is easy to throw him onto his back. In case of self-defense you can throw your man to the ground with such force that the back of his head will strike sufficiently hard to render him unconscious.

In practicing with a friend be careful at first not to use any undue violence. The student of Judo is taught from the very first how to fall and in a very few weeks can allow himself to be thrown by this method without suffering the slightest discomfort.

Lesson 6.

Judo students possess a formidable defense and offense against the assailant who leads a blow with his fist. Let us assume that an opponent has started a blow with his right fist at your stomach as in photo 1.

As the blow reaches toward you, strike his right elbow sharply with the flat of your left hand. This changes the course of the blow and sends your opponent spinning sidewise to your right. Simultaneously, grasp his right sleeve and pull him further in the direction he is spinning, as in photo No. 2.

This procedure will enable you to throw your right arm across his throat and get him from behind with your left in a neck lock, as in photo No. 3.

If deemed necessary the neck can be quickly broken with this hold.

On the other hand if thought advisable the person can be forced back-ward onto the ground and held helpless.

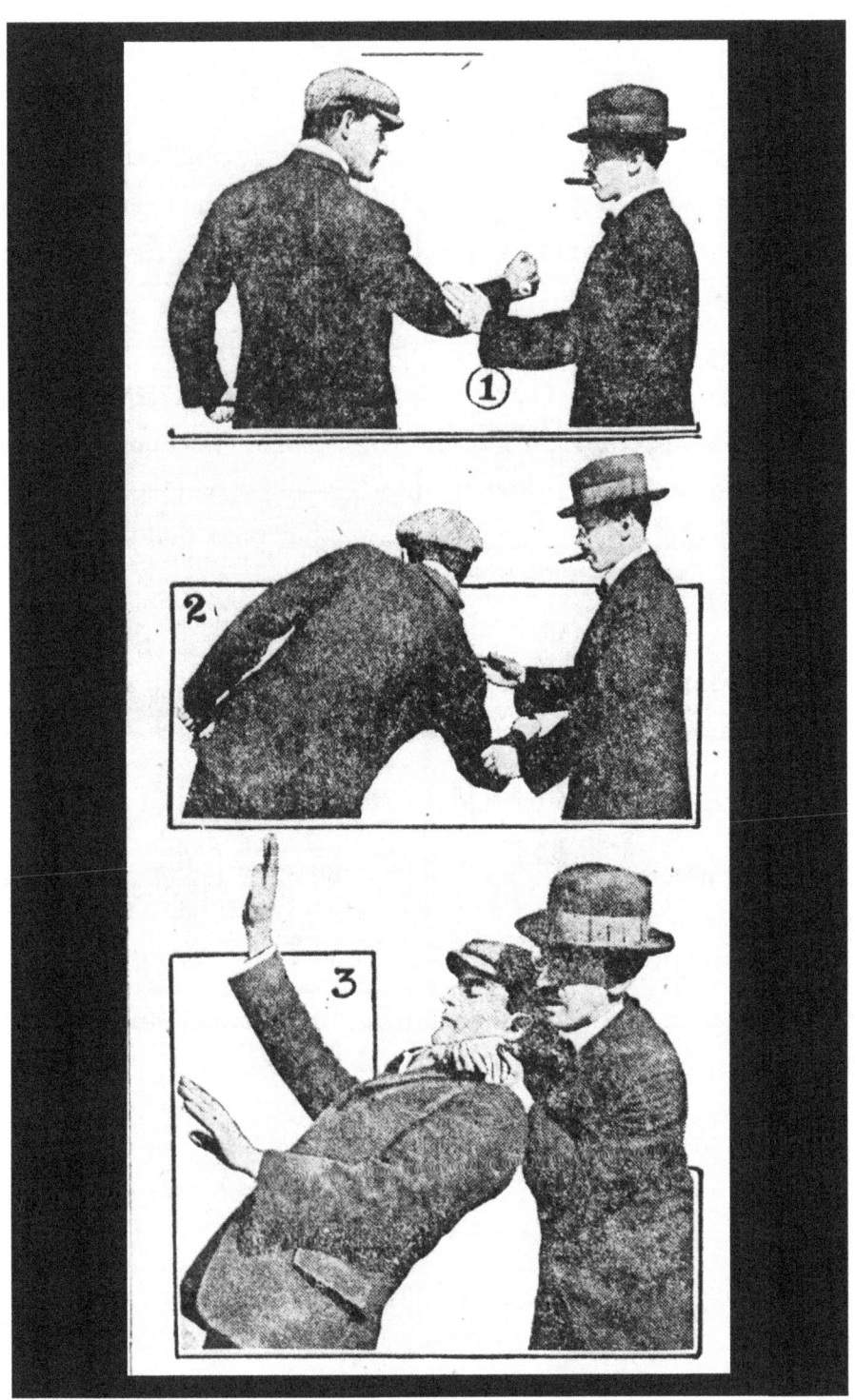

CAMP UPTON, LONG ISLAND

It was the same streamlined principles of Judo taught at Camp Upton and the other camps during WW1 that Smith would later go on to teach during WW2, later calling his program Battle Fighting.

An article in the **Brooklyn Daily Eagle** on Sunday, January 20th, describes Smith's time at Camp Upton while he was working there as a civilian aid to Major General Bell.

According to the article,
> If the truth is known there have been doubters as to the real worthwhileness of the gentle art of tearing a man's head from his shoulders, and from time to time these doubters have furnished Smith, the Stahara Kid, no end of fun. He weighs but 135 pounds, still he can handle a much larger man with laughable ease. In this latest development the Stahara Kid weighed a ton. He has frequently said in his lectures that there are many things about the art which are secret. It has been his boast that by the merest pressure of his finger on certain nerves he could render a man helpless.
>
> In one of his classes late yesterday afternoon was Lieutenant Philip M. Gray, Company C, 307th Infantry. Lieutenant Gray is a strapping big fellow. The Stahara Kid was demonstrating a strangle hold that makes Strangler Lewis look like a small boy.

The lieutenant, who was in peak condition, weighing over 200 pounds, grinned as he remarked that he did not think the Scot could put him out with the hold. It is a simple one - to look at. You simply take a man by the coat-collar on either side of the neck, with hands crossed, and apply the pressure. You really do a whole lot more, as the lieutenant learned, if you hold the Black Belt. The class was interested and urged the Stahara Kid to take up the dare. He consented finally.

He warned the man—*Remember: when the pressure becomes too great, clap your hands.*

Then he took hold. Gray withstood the terrific pressure like a hero. His face became flushed and the veins on his forehead stood out. It seemed as though the Stahara Kid was hoping to force the lieutenant to admit he could withstand the attack no longer. It was equally evident that the lieutenant would cut off own hands before he would clap them. Realizing he would have to put the man out, he shifted the grip just a trifle. Lieutenant Gray's face went white as chalk. The distended veins and eyes relaxed. His knees crumpled and he sank to the mat.

At this point, Smith who was the only calm person in the room smiled as he looked at the prone figure laying on the ground and then at the startled officers. *A little knowledge is dangerous*, he said. *He is not suffering but he is very much 'out,' as you Americans say. I will now apply a secret method of resuscitation and he will be back on his feet in an instant.*

Smith leaned over the lieutenant, seemed to fuss about his heart for a moment, and in a twinkling Lieutenant Gray was on his feet none the worse for wear.

Asked how he felt, Lt. Gray assured everyone that he was all right. *I did not suffer a bit after he shifted the grip. It was a pleasant, peaceful feeling that came over me.*

Smith would not tell how he brought the man back to consciousness. *It is a very old and a very secret method. One does not learn that until he has shown his right to wear the Black Belt. I simply manipulated certain nerve centers that act as a stimulant.*

One of the officers then remarked: *Suppose he put you out and then forgot to come back to 'anipulate certain nerve centers. That man gives me the creeps.*

In an article in the **Champaign Daily News,** Saturday, August 10th, titled ***Jiu-Jitsu Is Taught Yanks***, the reporter in Fort Myer, Virginia writes:

To see a class of 300 American soldiers learn, in one hour, ten different ways of *getting* a boche by jiu-jitsu gives one a great content.

It is so absurdly simple to kill a man without resorting to arms—if you know how!

Smith is the person teaching the Fort Myer rookies, *Remember, fellows,* he says, *this isn't the sort of fight you put up against a fair man in a fair fight. It's just the way to get a treacherous snake—a boche. Now follow me.*

For the purposes of the class, and similar to the Gray incident, Smith has a giant lieutenant and he looks like a pigmy in comparison.

Try to run me through with your bayonet, he says to the lieutenant—of course they don't use real bayonets in the class.

The lieutenant rushes Smith, there is a quick bending, a worming in, a sudden whirl, and the lieutenant falls with a whack on his back.

Observe, says Smith, *how easy it is to finish him.*

The next thing was to teach it, movement by movement, to the class, who were divided equally into *enemy* and *attacker.* It was difficult for the ones assigned to be "enemy" but in minutes the class had it down nicely and proceeded on to the next.

That day it was 90 in the shade and the average citizen would have collapsed. The reporter states that, *These 300 national army men, who yesterday were soft clerks, soda jerkers and newspaper reporters, came through like scratch men, which they are —and asked for more.*

Smith told the reporter "What these boys have learned today will mean life itself to many of them when they go over the top. A soldier trained in jiu-jitsu will have a supreme confidence, because he can defend himself absolutely against the unskilled enemy. Brute force is put at naught.

THE BATTLE FIGHTING COMBATIVES OF ALIAN C. SMITH

KOGIRO HANEISHI

An article in the **Brooklyn Daily Eagle** on January 29th, 1918, describes Allan Smith's assistant Haneishi as an inoffensive sort of a chap. It describes an incident where Lieutenant Percy L. Crosby, a cartoonist, and Lieutenant Marshall who had been taking lessons in the Jiu-Jitsu class decided to "get" the Japanese man for fun. The men were both exceptionally built and while neither was tall the article states that they had a trait known as "there." In other words, they could care for themselves.

When they jumped Haneishi he received no warning and before he knew what had happened he was on his back. According to the article it was all in good nature and the Japanese man was quick to see the point. The lieutenants applied holds and waited for him to clap his hand upon the mat as a signal of defeat.

Other officers in the class were watching the uneven contest with interest. There was a bit of a struggle and then Lieutenant Marshall sailed away from the mat and landed ten feet away in a corner. Crosby also sailed away to a distant part of the room and Haneishi rose from the mat and was smiling and calm. He had broken two exceedingly dangerous holds applied by strong men, with ease.

There was another incident in 1918 in which Haneishi had to prove his mettle in a contest at the camp with a Greek wrestler named Stiros Janatos.

The article describing the incident states that,
> As is the case in nearly every interesting development in camp the superiority of the Jap and his skill over brute strength grew out of some good-natured bantering. Smith is known among officers as the Stahara Kid. Not one of them can hold his own with him and it is commonly understood that he is a shade better than the Jap. Smith himself will tell anyone that Haneishi is a remarkable man and that it is about an even break between them.

> Instead of picking on Smith the officers declared in an off-hand manner that the Jap could not hold his own against a man they had discovered. To add insult to injury they declared their man weighted only 175 pounds. Haneishi weighs "one hun twen' fo," as he expresses it. It was agreed that the Jap would meet the

175-pounder and the match was arranged for yesterday afternoon in the Y.M.C.A. hut at Fifth avenue and First street.

The Y Administration Building and Auditorium at Camp Upton

Those who witnessed the contest will never forget it and those who failed to see it will forever wish they did. It is perhaps without a parallel in the history of sport. There have been matches between Jiu-Jitsu experts and wrestlers or boxers without number, and with varying results, but it is safe to say a Jiu-Jitsu expert never stacked up against the "plant" which waited for the Jap yesterday afternoon.

Present at the fight were Colonel W.R. Smedberg, commander of the 305th Infantry; Lieutenant Colonel Dolph, Major H. C. Woodward, First Lieutenant Loughborough, Lieutenant Colonel Ruben Smith,

Lieutenant Colonel A. Sloan of the 307th Infantry, Captain William D. Harrigan of Company I, 307th Infantry, and First Lieutenant McDermott of Company K, 307th Infantry, as well as several newspaper men.

It was Lieutenant Loughborough, who was the person who uncovered the soldier who would meet Haneishi. "He pulled a wonderfully well-built soldier aside and held a whispered conversation. He then told the gathering that Stiros Janatos, Company M. 305th infantry, whose home is at 554 State street, Brooklyn, would try his strength against the skill of the Jap."

Stiros then pulled off his shirt, shoes and socks. Even though he weighed 175 pounds, "he sure did look like an honest ton. His muscles bulged all over the place." Reminiscent of old time strongmen like the Mighty Atom Joseph Greenstein, Stiros then took a long iron poker and twisted it into hoops and loops. He then drove a heavy spike into a pine board with his fist and broke the spike off with his teeth. While he was doing all of those feats of strength he glared over at Haneishi.

"The Jap calmly witnessed the feats of strength and smoked his cigarette. When Stiros the Strong—and he is strong—had finished his exhibition the Jap clapped his hands."

Haneishi then said, "Strong—wonderful strong—magnificent specimen. Honorable Soldier, shake hands." Stiros grinned and shook hands.

Smith, who spoke in Japanese instructed Haneishi not to kill the Greek and then explained his instructions to those about him. There was a laughter and it was apparent that everyone in the room but Haneishi felt sorry for Haneishi.

Stiros who did not understand English well unless it was spoken slowly had a friend with him who acted as a translator. "He was to keep the Jap from making him "quit" and was to make the Jap quit. Only biting, gouging, striking with the fists and kicking were to be barred. In other words he could use the hammerlock, the head hold, the toe hold and the strangle hold—he could also choke to his heart's content."

As they faced each other, Stiros measured Haneishi and Haneishi in a matter-of-fact manner walked in and caught him by his wrist. "In a flash Stiros caught hold of him and they fell to the straw mats—the Jap on top. He had a hold which was difficult to see from the ringside. Nearly a minute elapsed and then Haneishi spoke excitedly in Japanese."

Smith translated for him "He says the Greek will be unconscious in a minute." Smith then pulled Stiros off and helped him to his feet. He was not unconscious but looked ill

They faced one another again. "Now thoroughly aroused to the contest the Greek began to exert his phenomenal strength. The Jap was a very busy man.

"He whirled and wriggled like a serpent. In fact, he resembled nothing more than an adder—deadly and swift. Again the Greek was forced to give in or be choked. All the time Stiros was fighting to put on a crushing hold. He found one difficult to get and his strength waning before it could be made effective.:

The reporter makes a point that ample safeguards were in place to protect both men, however there was something that appeared gruesome about the exhibition. "It is not nice to think what the little Jap could do to the average member of the Seventy-seventh Division."

They fought a third time. Spiros "is made of the stuff that wins battles and decides the fate of nations. He was whipped. He knew it, but his stout heart did not fail him." The reporter goes on to say "it was evident that Haneishi was about to show something. The Greek with his gigantic strength tossed him about like a feather. Suddenly the Jap stooped and gave a tug. Stiros was hurled through the air and landed flat on his back. Before he could move, before even the spectators had time to grasp the fact that the Greek had sailed through the air, Haneishi was across the mat with the speed of a tiger. He threw himself upon the heavier and stronger man. There was a whirl of figures and then both men lay still. The Jap had obtained an arm hold that left the strong man powerless."

Smith then said "With that hold in effect, the Greek is helpless. If he struggles he will break his arm and shoulder. The only way he could possibly escape would be to pull the member off at the shoulder."

That remark ended the exhibition. Haneishi had demonstrated that strength and courage were useless against the uncanny skill of the Jap. "The Greek, a fighter in his heart, was reluctant to admit defeat. He was a good sportsman and acknowledged his inability to cope with the other man under the conditions then existing. He wanted to meet the Jap with both men stripped to the waist."

Haneishi then said, "To the death, yes—no oth'" and it appeared that he meant it. After a moment of consideration, Stiros grinned and asked if he might take instruction in the art. Smith told him to come as often as he could manage.

The he turned to the spectators and said "You men now have some idea of what our ancient and honorable art consists of. You may also gather some idea of what my exhibitions with the Jap have been. I fought my way through hundreds of contests during the eleven years I labored to win the Black Belt. So did he. I never met a better man."

After the fight was over Lieutenant Loughborough the man who found Janatos for the bout said in disbelief "That fellow was with a big circus as a strong man and he claims to be the strongest man of his weight in the world."

"Three, four, six times as strong as Haneishi," was the Japanese Black Belt's reply.

It's not known at what point Haneishi and Smith went their separate ways. In 1919, Haneishi who had been stationed at several camps during the war, arrived at the University of Illinois to join the coaching staff.

He had come to the University from the Infantry School of Arms at Camp Benning, Georgia. G. Huff, the director of athletics saw him at work at Camp Benning and offered him the position.

Men enrolled in the athletic coaching school would receive instruction in Jiu-Jitsu from Haneishi, he also helped to coach the wrestling squad.

COURSE	CREDITS	SECTION	TITLE	HOUR	DAY	ROOM & BUILDING	INSTRUCTOR
ASSYRIAN—SECOND SEMESTER (See Oriental Languages and Literature.)							
ASTRONOMY—SECOND SEMESTER							
Astron. 2	3		General Astronomy	2	MWF	229 N. H.	Stebbins
Astron. 3	3		Navigation		Arrange		Stebbins
Astron. 14	3		Observational Astronomy		Arrange		Stebbins
Astron. 102	1 unit		Stellar Astronomy		Arrange		Stebbins
ATHELETIC COACHING AND PHYSICAL EDUCATION—SECOND SEMESTER							
A. C. 3	4		Free Exercise	10, 10, 11	MWFS TT	Gym.	Schuettner
A. C. 14	3		Hygiene	8	MWF	247 N. H.	Beard
A. C. 18[1]	1		Ju Jitsu	11	WFS	Gym.	Haneishi
A. C. 21	2		Track	2	MTWT	Armory and Ill. Field	Gill

[1]Open only to students taking Athletic Coaching.

**Course information for Haneishi's Ju Jitsu class at the University of Illinois.
Note: Only open to students taking Athletic Coaching**

BENNY LEONARD

The boxing instructor who was assigned to Camp Upton by the War Department was Benny Leonard, a well-known fighter, who was assisted by other men skilled in boxing.

He often gave frequent exhibitions at the Y.M.C.A. and Knights of Columbus huts at the camp. There were sparring exhibitions in which would-be champions were his opponents and he offered demonstrations of attack and defense in which the principles of bayonet fighting were involved.

Boxing As An Aid to Bayonet Practice

BENNY LEONARD, IN HIS SOLDIER'S UNIFORM.

Benny Leonard, world's lightweight champion, is in Uncle Sam's service. He will teach the soldier boys the art of self-defense in one of the training camps. Benny has already received his appointment as a boxing director, but he has not yet received his assignment. The photograph is the first showing him in his uniform.

The boxing directors are being selected with great care, only the best men are being appointed to train the soldiers.

Not only was Boxing considered to be an excellent form of exercise, but it was an aid to bayonet practice, it taught agility of the mind, disregard for personal injury and other elements associated with successful bayonet fighting.

"LIFTERS" AND "JABS" IN BAYONET AND BOXING WORK ARE DEMONSTRATED

Bennie Leonard, the boxing coach at Camp Upton, and Lieut. E. J. Statler demonstrating the similarity of "lifters" and "jabs" in boxing and bayonet work.

In an article in the **Atlanta Constitution,** January 9th, 1921, Benny states—

"I learned about the importance of understanding physiology while I was in the army. While I was boxing instructor at Camp Upton Lieutenant Smith was instructor in Jiu-Jitsu, which he learned in Japan. We worked together and he taught me Jiu-Jitsu. I learned a lot of things about the nerves and the vital organs."

"Do you know what a knock-out is? It's simply a shock to a nerve, carried to the brain. There are three knock-out points on the head, each where nerves lie near the surface. For instance, a straight blow on the end of the chin isn't a good knock-out punch. But hit a man on either side of the chin, an inch or so back, or above the eye tooth, and you deliver a shock to the nerve connecting with the brain. The nerve telegraphs the brain that you're knocked out, and down you go. A Jiu-Jitsu expert can put a man out by digging at certain nerves with his thumb. It isn't necessary to deliver a smashing blow."

The Battle-Fighting Combatives of Allan Corstorphin Smith
Book II

SOME BACKGROUND ON 10 WAYS TO GET A BOCHE

In 1918 while stationed at Camp Upton, Long Island, in an unpublished training document **10 Ways to "Get" A Boche**, Allan Smith expands on his training program which started initially with the six newspaper articles he published.

In an article in the **Boston Globe,** June 30th, 1918 titled 10 *Ways To Get A Boche, Taught By Jiu Jitsu Experts*, there is a description of the program Smith teaches the troops along with Haneishi. All of the articles about Smith and Haneishi have the same sort of theme which puts one under the impression that Smith and his assistant taught the courses in pretty much the same format every time, the biggest student of the bunch is selected to perform a technique on and due to the size and strength of the student one assumes that the technique cannot be performed and the student will get the best of the teacher however in almost every instance the student is unable to overcome the teacher. This article starts off the same way, however it goes into some detail about the War Department's decision to request that Jiu Jitsu be taught alongside Boxing and Wrestling in the camps.

"They tell a story, which may be only a story, of an attempt to convince the War Department about 10 years ago that jiu jitsu might be useful. Three Japs wanted to teach it. They told the War Department to pick out three of the huskiest men in its army and the War Department did, three giants with fighting reputations.

"The three soldiers and the three Japs met in combat, and without soaring preliminaries the soldiers rushed. *Biff! Biff! Biff!* Each soldier swung once with his trusty right and the three Japs took the count. And Jiu-Jitsu wasn't adopted then.

"So that story goes. But nothing has happened here this week to bear out the plausibility of the story.

"It is a record of history, however, that Japan summoned every Jiu-Jitsu instructor in its realms at the outbreak of the Russo-Japanese War and sent them into the army to teach.

"Jiu-Jitsu had been a pastime indulged in only by the Samurai, the warrior class of old Japan. And when Japan came to conscript its army under modern conditions it had an army made up of the three "lower classes" as it regarded them, the farmers, the artisans and the merchants—in that order. The Government was querulous as the spirit of that army.

"'We'll teach them Jiu-Jitsu,' said the Government. 'That gives men supreme confidence. It will give them *Yamato Damashi*, 'the Spirit of Japan.' Physically the Russians were so much bigger and stronger than the Japs: and in hand-to-hand fighting without arms many a Russian was killed by the cunning use of hands and feet by the Japanese."

I have included Smith's pamphlet here. It shows his system. He used concepts of this system again later on in World War Two. It is a bare-bones, simplified system of hand-to-hand combat, as it should be. Easy to learn, easy to retain and effective.

Joseph E. Raycroft in his book, **Mass Physical Training** *for use in The Army and the Reserve Officer's Training Corps,* describes it this way: "Emphasis should be placed upon the fact that hand-to-hand fighting is to be regarded as an emergency measure and that it is to be resorted to only when ordinary weapons of offence and defense are not available.

"A soldier should always depend upon his rifle, bayonet or grenade as his best means of offense and defense. This idea should be thoroughly drilled into the men."

However, if any of those are not available,
> "The holds that are described have been selected from a very large number of hand-to-hand combinations, because experience has shown that they are best adapted to secure effective results when used by men in full equipment upon opponents equipped with helmet, gas mask, pack, etc. Many holds that are effective in the absence of equipment and with only one opponent have been discarded as useless under service conditions when the men are handicapped by full equipment and by rough, muddy ground.

"The spirit of hand-to-hand fighting is that of grim, watchful determination. The men must be trained to keep on their feet and to avoid going to the ground with their opponents. They should be taught to use the kick, the knee, and the elbow whenever possible and to cultivate speed and accuracy in taking holds. Aggressiveness and determination in making attack are invaluable as a means of putting and keeping the opponent on the defense.

"Principles of sportsmanship and consideration for your opponent have no place in the practical application of this work. In a fight with a bigger, stronger man avoid aimless struggle but work deliberately to disable or disconcert him by butting with head, kicking shins, grabbing gas mask, etc., so as to make an opening for a disabling hold or blow.

"It is to be noted that the knee, crotch, neck, and head are vulnerable parts and are the object of attack."

In the article Smith says, "If it ever comes to a showdown, you've got your man." It is that feeling which Jiu-Jitsu provides. Such confidence is worth months of training. You may be a hundred yards away sniping your enemy with a rifle, but you know you're his master in a close encounter and that makes one feel in control. And that was the reason why jiu jitsu was being adopted for No Man's Land on the western front. It was one of the new things—as old as the hills—adapted for the most modern of wars. Like the buckshot shotgun.

Smith says, "A man is trained not only in aggressiveness, but is made to feel that as the result of his training he is a better warrior physically, mentally, and spiritually, than his enemy."

ROUGH STUFF FOR HEINIES WHO MEET OFFICERS OF 82ND F. A.

New System of Hand-to-Hand Fighting Now Being Taught at Fort Bliss; All Soldiers at Fort to Be Instructed In Tactics For Close Quarters; Officers Go After Each Other In Real Earnest In Practice.

Officers of the 82d field artillery, Brig. Gen. H. P. Howard, commanding, have been hardened to some trying stunts within the last two weeks, but hand to hand fighting, taken up this morning at 7 o'clock under supervision of Capt. John R. Bender, proved the most exciting athletic training yet taken by them.

Pairing off in two's under instructions the officers were taught the proper and effective way to choke a German soldier. It was a novel sight to see the officers springing at each other and give their most intensive choking efforts on a brother officer. The counter for choking—the favorite stunt of German soldiers in close quarters—proved even more interesting.

Proper Method.

On the offensive the soldier grasps the throat of an opponent with both hands, brings knee hard to crotch and stepping in trips and throws opponent. While the throat hold is broken in a number of ways, the one employed in beginning—and believed to be most effective, especially among those who understand boxing—is to bring the extended right arm forcibly over to the left, jerking opponent forward, at same time striking blow with elbow, followed with wrist to the neck. This may be followed with a left hook.

All the fundamental holds used in attack and breaks for the same will be taken up by the officers and afterwards by the enlisted men of the 82d field artillery.

The same tactics in similar form have been taken previously by the officers and men of the Seventh cavalry, Fifth cavalry, recruit camp and others.

Civilians Should Learn.

There is a general movement throughout the country for high school students and civilians of military age to take up and practice the hand to hand fighting, the fundamental holds of which are given below. Preparation in anticipation of military service greatly helps when men go to the training camps and cantonments, and those who will begin on the following, mastering each before taking on a new one, shall have begun his preparation to banish the Hun once and for all.

The instructions in short, follow:

Hand To Hand Fighting Program.

1. Front Throat Attack—Grasp throat with both hands, circle thumbs about windpipe; follow with knee to fork and leg trip to ground.

Break—(a). Swing right arm over opponent's breaking his hold; drive elbow or forearm to jaw or side of neck.

(b). Grasp opponent's wrist and twist outward at the same time reach under his arm and grasp his shoulder and trip to ground.

2. Front Body Attack—Clasp both arms about waist, press chin to the chest, pull in and bend back, leg trip, fall and put knee to ribs or fork.

Break—Press thumbs into his eyes or under his nose.

3. Front Body Attack—Place one arm to small of back, pull forward and put heel of hand to his chin, drive knee to fork, leg trip.

Break—Turn head slightly, knock off his elbow and use same attack.

4. Front Leg Attack—Opponent charges high, crouch quickly, step in and lift his forward leg, advance other foot and trip him, fall with knee to fork and regain feet and stamp and kick him.

Break—(a). Use double stiff arms to shoulders and pull his face to knee.

5. Take front strangle, or use point of elbow to head.

5. Front Arm Attack—(a). Cross arm palm or wrist grasp, pull quickly forward and throw your left arm inside and under his right and press down.

(b). Same grasp, pull quickly forward and throw your left arm under his right arm; grasp his shirt at the neck and twist, press down.

(c). Same grasp, pull quickly forward at the same time turn and throw your left arm across his throat and trip with left leg.

(d). Same grasp, pull quickly forward, turn and put his elbow palm up on your shoulder and break arm.

6. Knife Defence—(a). Opponent strikes down with knife in right hand. Grasp his wrist with left hand, step in quickly with right foot and put your right arm under his right elbow, grasp his wrist and break arm.

(b). Opponent strikes up with knife in right hand. Grasp his wrist, step in, put your arm under his shoulder and hip lock him to the ground. Retain wrist hold, put knee under his elbow and break arm.

(c). Opponent strikes up, step to the left quickly, grasp wrist with left hand, grasp his knife hand with your right, pull down, he will resist, then swing his arm and only over your left shoulder and knee to fork.

7. Rear Strangle—Grasp shoulders, pull backward and drive foot at the same time against opponent's knee, take strangle hold forearm across the throat, place your head alongside his and press down and push up.

Break: Grasp elbow, drop quickly to ground and throw over shoulder.

8. Rear Body Hold—Arm about waist and crotch hold, lift and throw to ground, follow with leg kick to ribs, face and crotch or kidneys.

Break—Grasp wrists drive heel to shin or instep, then follow with head smash to face, stoop quickly, lift leg, turn and kick.

9. Rear Leg Attack—Grasp ankle, push him down and apply leg kicks.

10. Ground Defence—Turn on side, hook under foot back of his forward foot and kick to knee with your other foot. If you miss this hold keep kicking him off and regain feet as soon as possible.

Article in the *El Paso Herald*, Tuesday October 15th, 1918

THE
BATTLE FIGHTING
COMBATIVES OF
ALIAN C. SMITH

Introduction

What is the best manner of developing the fighting spirit in a soldier?

This is a question that has been a potent one with military experts since the early days of civilization. Even savages have recognized its importance. The American Indian cultivated courage by self-torture. The Spartan conception of nourishing a fighting spirit was by means of physical culture carried to extremes.

The games of Ancient Rome were for the purpose of bringing the fighting spirit to the fore. Similarly were the tournaments held in the days of chivalry.

But in no wars of history has the scientific side of developing "the will to fight" been studied as carefully as in the present one. For years soldiers of the German Army have been trained on the theory that mere brute strength develops such a will.

Since the Battle of the Marne, the English military experts have sought to develop in the soldiers of Great Britain an aggressive spirit combined with initiative effort, chiefly through bayonet work. The French have steadfastly, since the terrible losses of Verdun, followed the theory that "You cannot fight with men against material" In other words, they have tried to make invention and machinery supersede brute strength. They have resorted to hand grenades and automatic rifles instead of bayonets.

To my mind the best method of developing the fighting spirit is being followed in the Japanese Army. Here the individual is trained, not only in aggressiveness, but is made to feel that as the result of his training he is a better warrior physically, mentally and spiritually, than his enemy.

The foundation of his training is "Jiu-jitsu," which translated into English means "the art of yielding." In other words this is the art of overcoming physical superiority by appearing to yield to it. If you are stronger than your opponent, so much the better, provided you understand Jiu-jitsu. If you are weak physically, you may overcome a giant who knows how to use his muscles only as a brute.

Having lived in Japan for 12 years and studied "Jiu-jitsu" during all of that time, I know whereof I write. On January 9th, 1916, the Central College of Jiu-jitsu of Tokio awarded me the certificate of teacher. A very solemn ceremony took place. Officers of the Japanese Army and Navy were present. The certificate entitled me to teach this noble art in Japan, and I acted as Assistant Instructor in the Kodokan at Tokio, the greatest Jiu-jitsu school in the world.

While in Japan I saw soldiers of the Japanese Army taking Jiu-jitsu as part of their military training. The Japanese used Jiu-jitsu effectually in the war with Russia, and many cases are recorded in which Japanese soldiers killed Russians with their bare hands. Jiu-jitsu is the ideal form of physical training for trench warfare.

It is the "exercise of surprises" and at the same time is "Cave man" fighting par excellence. In Jiu-jitsu any sort of blow or hold is considered fair. The whole substance of it is, "Get your man before he gets you." It makes no difference how you "get" him.

As to its application, the Germans do not care a snap of their fingers how they "get" the Allies. With them it is, "Kick your man when he is down; grind your heel in his face—anything."

In Jiu-jitsu it is "Get your man off his balance, surprise and overpower him by a quick and unexpected move—and then do with him as you please."

Jiu-jitsu is peculiarly fitted to the American fighter. It requires speed, agility, quick thinking. Its own results tend to strengthen the self-confidence and courage of the man who masters this art. The English Army has taken to Jiu-jitsu. Police Departments all over the world are using it. I am teaching the art to American soldiers at Camp Upton.

After giving a few lessons to American soldiers I was delighted to see them practicing in their barracks during their spare time. Their interest and the serious manner with which they studied the various holds, convinced me that Jiu-jitsu is adapted to the American temperament.

Furthermore, it is a form of physical training that fit a man to fight with or without firearms. It instills self-confidence. Self-confidence breeds courage; and courage and the indomitable will to win in a just cause develop a "will to fight" that is unconquerable. This and this only is the will that spells utter defeat for Germany.

What is the first step toward proficiency in Jiu-jitsu? Developing the stahara. What is the stahara?

Stahara is the Japanese name for that part of the abdomen which lies beneath the navel. The Stahara is the most important part of the fighting man. It is here the center of gravity lies, and it is by controlling the stahara that you master the emotions of fear and courage. In plain English, *stahara* means just courage - courage for a fight as well as strong stomach muscles.

By the usual method of teaching Jiu-jitsu it takes years to get the knack of using the stahara properly, but by the specific exercises given to the soldiers at Camp Upton they are able to use the stahara intelligently in a few weeks.

Test for Efficiency of Stahara

Assume an exaggerated military position, chest arched to its fullest extent, stomach drawn in, chin drawn in. Now let someone take your coat collar between forefingers and thumbs and pull you forward, and note how easily you lose your balance. This is because there is no strength in the stahara.

Now stand in a naturally erect position, and concentrate your strength in the stahara, and again let him pull you forward and you will find that you are at least twice as strong.

This is because the stahara is full of strength. This illustration demonstrates one of the fundamental principles of Jiu-jitsu, which is that whether wrestling or fighting with a weapon, you must have your mind concentrated on your stahara.

First Stahara Exercise

Stand with the heels two feet apart, bring the fists up in front of the chest, elbows at the sides, and strike out as if making an uppercut but without moving the arms, that is, throw the head back and the stahara forward, bending the knees and bringing them well forward. When in this position the abdominal muscles should be hard and tense like a wash-board.

Second Exercise for Strengthening the Stahara

The following exercise if practiced regularly will give you the knack of making a strong effort from the stahara.

Stand with the heels about two feet apart, bend down as if to lift a heavy bar bell, and raise it to the waist, putting no effort into the arms or legs, but solely into the stahara.

Persons with a tendency toward hernia ought not do this exercise. If you are not used to violent exercise start this movement moderately at first. Done properly, the muscles of your stahara will feel sore for the first week or so, but this is a good sign.

Exercise for Continual Control of Stahara

Stand erect, take a deep breath and harden the abdomen as much as possible, not merely with the superficial muscles, but with the downward internal pressure. Sink the center of gravity as much as possible, in other words try to make your belt tight.

Exhale deeply and again harden the stahara with the internal downward pressure. This is the same exercise as you get in the regular stahara drill.

Try to practice this exercise wherever you are, standing, walking or sitting, and without letting anyone know what you are doing. In other words, your face must be impassive, or smiling, while doing this exercise. A little practice will enable you to harden the stahara to a remarkable degree.

Your efforts will be directed at first solely towards bearing down, towards "making the belt tight," as it were. But, as the control increases, you will also contract the muscles of the stahara, that is, that part of the abdomen lying beneath the navel. When the control is properly acquired, there are two factors at work, first a downward pressure from the diaphragm, secondly an upward pressure from the stahara.

After one or two days' practice you will find that you are able to breathe noiselessly, even while taking deep and rapid breaths, and once this control is acquired, always breathe this way in the future. You will also of course always breathe through the nostrils with the mouth shut.

Take fifty deep breaths in this manner every morning upon arising, and for the first month practice this exercise as much as possible during the day. After the end of the month deep breathing and the control of the stahara will be more or less a habit, and this habit you should cultivate as long as you take a keen interest in living – and putting up a good, stiff fight for your country.

Balance

Once the stahara control is properly mastered, you feel that you have a private gyroscope working in your abdomen and this will enable you to keep your balance and prevent yourself being knocked over.

To illustrate, stand up and lift up your right foot and untie and retie the shoe lace. You will perhaps find some difficulty in maintaining your balance, but concentrate upon the stahara while you are doing this and you will find you are able to retain your balance easily.

Limbering Up Exercise

Bring the right knee up to the height of the waist dropping the left knee a couple of inches, thus lowering the center of gravity slightly. Concentrate all your strength in the stahara and limber up your lower leg by moving it backward and forward quickly. Imagine that you have a rifle and bayonet in your hand and that you are ready to strike either with that weapon or with your foot. Practice this for ten seconds and then change to your left foot and so on alternately.

The Kick

The Jiu-jitsu kick can be done much more swiftly than an ordinary kick. In aiming a kick at an enemy's crotch, as your toe flies out, bring your knee up to the height of your waist. This will result in the toe landing on the desired point a great deal quicker than by the ordinary method. At the same time lower the center of gravity by dropping the other knee a couple of inches, and concentrate your strength in the stahara.

Get someone to push your shoulder while you make a kick in the old-fashioned way and he will send you staggering backwards. Then let him push you again after you have mastered this method of kicking and you will find his push has no effect on you.

With the aid of these notes any soldier who has been in one of my classes will be able to train himself to deliver this kick quickly and effectively.

The Real Secret of Fighting

Most of the Jiu-jitsu tricks shown in this book are methods of releasing yourself from an enemy's grip, and you must continually train yourself until you can do them automatically. This is not only because they may save your life in an emergency, but for the reason that they will show you that science is superior to strength and will train you in time to be afraid of no man.

Never attack an enemy with the idea of getting one of these holds on him. For the aggressive, you must train yourself to think of attacking like a whirlwind with the toe, knee, elbow and heel of hand. Get in at him and keep pressing him, but instead of grabbing him, kick him on the spots shown you, knock his head back with the blows shown you and keep it up till you have him on the ground.

These methods never are to be resorted to in a fair fight against a fair man - only against an unscrupulous, treacherous foe. Now for the ten ways to "get" the boche. These are secrets, some of which never before have been published. They are given with the idea of helping to make our American army victorious in the most desperate war known to history.

First Way

Seized Round Waist From Front (1)

A favorite method of a bully is to rush at you, seize you round the waist, bend your back in and force you to the ground. As your opponent rushes forward, step inside his grip and place the heel of your right hand below his chin. Be sure to have your forearm perpendicular on his chest. The reason is that if your elbow sticks out you have only the strength of the shoulder muscles (the deltoids) with which to push back his head. If your forearm is straight up and down, however, you can make the effort from the stahara, that is, you can push up your arm with the whole weight of the body behind it. Another reason is, that if you aim at his chin and miss it, your effort miscarries, whereas by striking in this way if you miss his chin you still catch his nose.

Slip your left arm round your opponent's waist just where his belt is, and pull his waist towards you. By doing this you upset his balance and it is just as important to pull his waist towards you as it is to push his chin away from you.

So that this may be practiced without injury it is done in two counts: (1) place your right hand beneath his chin and your left arm around his waist, (2) draw his waist towards you with the left hand and push his head back with your right. In actual warfare the whole movement would be executed with one swift stroke.

In practicing this at first, do not make it a wrestling contest, but the attacked party will let the attacker execute this movement on him without resistance and after several trials reverse the positions, the attacker in turn becoming the attacked. You must practice in this manner with at least a dozen different opponents until you get the proper knack of doing it with the minimum exertion of strength on the biggest and strongest man you can find.

Chin Hold

Second Way

Seized Round Waist From Front (2)

Suppose your opponent has seized you round the waist so unexpectedly and quickly that you are unable to get the chin hold on him and that he is now commencing to bend you backward on the ground. The first thing to do is to bring your knee quickly and forcibly under his crotch.

If he holds you so close that you are unable to bring your knee up, and if his chin is pressing into your chest, bring your thumb beneath his nose, press his head back until his hold on your waist breaks and his crotch becomes open to a blow from your knee, when you at once deliver it.

This movement is executed in three counts: (1) opponent seizes you around the waist, burying his chin on your chest and bending you over backwards; (2) bring your thumb beneath his nose and press his head back until his crotch is open to the knee blow; (3) bring up your knee to the desired position.

In practice with a friend be careful not to cause him injury through too vigorous a push on his nose or actually striking him forcibly on the crotch. Accuracy and speed in this movement will come from repeated practice, and self-confidence will be developed as a result of continually freeing yourself from the grip of stronger men, remembering always that in actual warfare you strike with your knee to kill and you deliver the push or the blow on the nose with enough vigor to break his neck by jerking his head back, and that if the first blow does not succeed in knocking your enemy out you must repeat these blows or alternate them until you have him lying on the ground helpless.

Escape From Waist Hold

Third Way

Attacked With Chin Hold

If an enemy should happen to take you at such disadvantage that he secures the chin hold, you can only extricate yourself from this position by Jiu-jitsu, in other words, by appearing to yield to his superior strength. Allow a friend to secure this chin hold on you and to hold you firmly with your waist pulled in towards him and you will find that you are helpless. Try to resist with the strength of your neck and you will find you are in danger of having your neck broken.

By the principle of Jiu-jitsu, however, as you find your head being pushed back by his hand, give way to his thrust, throw your head back quicker than he pushes it and at the same time knock up his hand.

To perform this movement correctly the effort must be made from the stahara, and as soon as your head has evaded his thrust you must regain the normal balanced position. Follow this instantaneously by a blow with the heel of your hand, either on his chin or his nose, jerking his head backwards and finishing the coup by the knee on his crotch.

If it is his right hand which is inserted beneath your chin you knock it up with your left hand in the following manner:

Bring your left elbow onto your abdomen and strike his arm with the heel of your hand, letting the strength come not from the muscles of your arm, but from your stahara. This does not mean that you are to leave the muscles of your arm limp, as, on the contrary, you will use the strength of your arm to its fullest extent, but by bringing the elbow in front of the body and by making the effort from the stahara you will more than double the power of the blow.

In practice this is done in four counts: (1) The front rank secures the chin hold on the rear rank; (2) front rank pushes rear rank's head back and pulls waist in, at the same time rear rank throws head back and knocks up the arm of front rank, and regains balanced position; (3) rear rank uses chin blow or nose blow with the heel of hand; (4) rear rank finishes with knee on crotch.

Enemy Gets Chin Hold

Escape From Chin Hold

Fourth Way

Attacked From Behind (1)

If an opponent seizes you from behind, throwing his arms round you, clasping them in front and pinning your arms to your side, the first essential is to hit him on the shin with the heel of your boot. The proper place is half way between the ankle and the knee on the edge of the bone. At this point, just where the muscle joins the bone, there is a peculiarly sensitive spot and a sharp blow here will do a great deal towards disturbing a man's nervous system.

If delivered with enough force and accuracy it may cause your opponent to drop to the ground and if your kick has this effect upon the enemy so much the better. In the method now under description the object of the kick is attained in the sudden weakening of your opponent. The immediate result of the kick will be that the strength of his grasp is greatly diminished.

You take immediate advantage of this by twisting your stahara to the left. Do not try to twist your shoulders round. If a man's arms are stronger than yours you would find great difficulty in turning if you oppose the strength of your arms to the strength of his arms, but if you leave your own arms and shoulders limp and turn strongly from the stahara the effect of the movement will be to twist your shoulders round.

You now drive your elbow into his solar plexus and he falls to the ground and if the trick has been correctly performed, he is knocked out.

Elbow on Solar Plexus

Fifth Way

Attacked From Behind (2)

If an opponent seizes you below the arms, if he is a strong man, you would have difficulty in getting away by ordinary methods. But your first care must be to weaken him by a vigorous kick delivered with the heel of your shoe in the middle of his shin, as described in the preceding method.

Alternately to the kick on the shin you may butt him on the face with the back of your head, the best place to catch him being on the nose. The object is to strike him so swiftly and vigorously that you momentarily weaken him and throw him off his guard.

No matter what strength your opponent may have, if you execute a kick or butt effectively you will find no difficulty in succeeding in the following method:

Grasp the front of his right breeches leg with your right hand and push vigorously, at the same time turning your stahara to the left, which will bring you into the position shown in picture captioned, "Grab enemy's leg." You should spend considerable time in mastering this move accurately, doing it slowly at first.

You will find even in friendly wrestling, where kicks on the shin are debarred, that you can escape from an ordinary man's grasp by this movement, but it is necessary that the effort be made with the stahara and that the push with the arm be performed simultaneously. In other words, it is a knack, which if properly acquired is easy of execution. But if the movement be not done correctly, mere strength of effort will not succeed.

Having twisted the body into the foregoing position, like a flash bring your fist up and hit your opponent a vicious jab below the belt. If done properly this should result in knocking him out.

To make doubly sure, however, you bring your right foot from in front of opponent round behind his left leg, knocking up his thigh with your knee, and throwing him back onto the ground by the pressure of your right elbow. This throw, performed properly, should cause his head to strike the ground with sufficient force to render him unconscious.

Grab Enemy's Leg

Throw Him

Sixth Way

Attempted Throttle

The enemy seizes you by the throat, pushing you backwards and burying his thumbs in your wind pipe. He may even cross his thumbs over your wind pipe, which is a still more serious position for you. At once bring your knee up onto his crotch. This should cause his collapse, but at least it will render the accomplishment of the following method easy for the weakest man when attacked by the strongest opponent:

Bring both elbows onto the abdomen and strike up his arms with the heels of your hands. This effort is made from the stahara, that is to say, you bring the stahara forward with as much force as possible, this in turn drives the heel of your hand against his arms, knocking them up. Simultaneously you throw your head back, jerking your throat out of his grasp. Immediately regain your balance, knock his head back with a blow from the heel of the hand beneath his chin, and follow with the knee blow on his crotch.

After mastering this movement, it is possible to free yourself from the strongest man's attempt to throttle you without the necessity of kicking him first, but it is necessary for the soldier to train himself to strike the enemy in a vital spot whenever he is close enough to do so. The Wrist-breaking-twist and the Elbow-break can also be used against a man who attempts to throttle you.

OVERCOMING ATTEMPTED THROTTLE

If Enemy Throttles You —

Escape And Regain Balance –

Then "Get" Him

Seventh Way

The Wrist Breaking Twist

Let a friend hold the back of his right hand towards you. Grasp him round the ball of the thumb with your left hand, your fingers covering the palm of his hand, your thumb resting on the middle of the back of his hand. Bring the ball of your right thumb over the ball of the left and the fingers of your right hand round the palm of this hand. Do not exert the strength of your fingers and thumbs but make the grip a clinging one.

From this position move his hand sideways and outwards, slowly and gradually, until your friend feels his wrist breaking, when he will give you the signal to stop, and you at once release him. Practice this until you can secure the grip without hesitation. Then let him turn the side of his hand toward you; continue practicing this grip; finally let him turn the palm of his hand toward you and continue practicing until here again you can secure the correct grip without a second's hesitation, then practice securing the same grip on his other hand. You must not expect to master this grip without a good deal of conscientious practice.

Now, you never tackle a man with the object of securing this hold, for if your opponent is stronger than you he would at once perceive your object and prevent your getting the grip. The opportunity to use it comes when a strong man grasps you. You then utilize the strength he is exerting to bring about his own defeat.

For instance, if he attempts to throttle you, knock up his left hand only with your right hand, bring your left fingers on the ball of his right thumb and your thumb on the back of his hand, as described above, and hold his hand firmly against your shoulder, at the same time turn your body quickly to the left. This will have the effect of straightening his right arm and pulling him slightly off his balance. The moment your right hand has succeeded in knocking his left hand from your throat it instantly takes its share of the wrist-breaking-hold on your opponent's right hand and assists in pressing his hand firmly against your own shoulder. Now turn his wrist as described above, but do so by turning your body, thus, even if his right arm is stronger than the combined strength of both of your arms you could still defeat him, because you are using the strength of your body, which, of course, is greater than the strength of his arm.

Similarly, if he seizes you by the clothing, the collar, or the lapels of your coat, if you have the proper knack of this trick you can easily make him a helpless prisoner. To properly master this trick requires long and conscientious practice, on every conceivable style of opponent. If you fail at times to apply this grip properly do not attempt to succeed by using more strength, but do the trick more slowly and try to analyze your faults, also get someone who can do this trick to watch you and advise you. Do not attempt speed until you have accuracy.

Breaking Enemy's Wrist

Eighth Way

The Elbow Break

Seize a man's left wrist with both hands, take a step back with your left foot, pulling his shoulder forward. In order to get this movement correct at first, your opponent must stand still until you get the knack of pulling him off his balance. Once you have acquired the knack of unbalancing a stationary opponent you may combine it with footwork. That is, if your opponent takes a step forward to maintain his balance, you step back in the same direction quickly and just that much farther than he to make him lose his balance.

Once you have acquired the knack of unbalancing a stationary opponent you may combine it with footwork. That is, if your opponent takes a step forward to maintain his balance, you step back in the same direction quickly and just that much farther than he to make him lose his balance. Having unbalanced him, and having pulled his upper right arm down to a level with your shoulder (we are presuming your opponent is a much taller man than you), take a step forward with your right foot and bring your right armpit over his left upper arm and press it downward with the weight of your body, making the effort from the stahara and keeping your body perfectly erect.

It is not necessary to twist his arm. Your left hand simply holds his left wrist naturally, with his little finger uppermost, pulling it evenly towards your face. By now gradually increasing the pressure of your upper right arm it will cause enough pain to make him surrender.

Do not apply the pressure with a jerk, but put it on evenly. The test of success in this trick is that you hold your opponent so helpless that he is unable to make any attack upon your crotch with his free hand.

Having mastered this method by gradual practice, you must again be cautioned never to tackle a man with the object of securing this hold on him. But if he, for instance, attempts to throttle you, or takes hold of the lapel of your coat you will then have an opportunity for securing this hold. It may also be used to take prisoner a man who has seized your wrists.

**If the Enemy Seizes You by the Throat,
Step Back, Unbalancing Him on the Way –**

and Put Him in Your Power in this Manner

Ninth Way

Stalking a Sentry Noiselessly

You are crawling up behind a German sentry in the dark. If you do not get him he will get you. Furthermore, if, in getting him, he cries out or gives the alarm you allow him to summon his comrades and, what is worse, you alarm the whole enemy's line. The following method will not only enable you to get him in a grip by which you can either break his neck and kill him, or hold him a helpless prisoner, but it should also enable you to prevent his making any sound:

Let us suppose that he is a much taller man than you. You steal up behind him, raise your knee to the height of his hips and place your hands just over his shoulders. Drive his hips suddenly forward with your knee and simultaneously jerk his shoulders back. This will cause him to topple backwards.

Properly performed this movement takes only a fraction of a second. The point is that you pull his shoulders straight backwards and knock his hips forward. If you practice until you get the proper knack of this you will find that it requires no strength to topple the largest man over.

While he is still falling backward you bring the sharp, bony part of your right wrist as hard as you can against his "Adam's apple." This action follows so swiftly upon the former that he has not yet had time to call out, and this blow on the wind pipe will effectually deprive him of the use of his voice.

Your right wrist remains where it is, pulling him backwards, and in conjunction with the neck hold secures a grip upon his head, which, by the time he hits the ground, has put him absolutely in your power.

The neck lock must first be practiced on a friend who sits on the ground and allows you to try it repeatedly on him until you can put it on him without hesitation.

Bring your right wrist across his throat, keeping your wrist rigid and straight. Place your left elbow on his shoulder close to his neck, the hook of the elbow being a line with the point of his jaw. Put the fingers of your right hand on the upper arm just at the elbow, and bring the palm of your left hand behind his head. Press his head forward with the palm of your left hand and strangle him with the edge of your right wrist.

In practicing this with a friend be careful not to put it on violently or with a jerk, and when it becomes effective let him clap his hands as a signal of defeat, when you will at once let go. Raise your arms above your head and bring them down and take the hold again, swiftly but gently. When you have got the proper knack combine it with the trick of toppling over a sentry.

To avoid injury it is practiced in class to three counts: (1) Place your knee behind his hips and your hands on his shoulders; (2) shoot your knee forward and your hands back, but instead of bringing your wrist across his "Adam's apple" bring it onto his chest, and instead of bringing the left elbow over his shoulder slip the left hand under his armpit, and lower him to the ground; (3) after he is on the ground put the neck hold on him.

By this method of practicing all chance of injury is eliminated, and you can become an expert in the art of lowering a large man quickly to the ground, and there quickly putting the neck hold on him, remembering that in actual warfare you put the neck hold on him the moment his shoulders come on a level with your own. This lock can be secured in such a way that his spine will snap with the impact of his body on the ground. There is a still more efficacious and secret way of breaking a man's spine which is communicated only in class.

How to Stalk a Sentinel

Tenth Way

Jiu-jitsu and the Bayonet

Jiu-jitsu is not offered as a substitute for the bayonet, but as a supplement to it. Apart from the fact that the Jiu-jitsu kick is much quicker than the ordinary kick, a soldier who makes a kick in the ordinary way might unfortunately choose to make it just at the moment his enemy was in a position to throw him off his balance. A Jiu-jitsu man, however, is not only quite balanced himself when he makes a kick, but he contrives to throw his adversary off his balance while making it.

When fighting with a bayonet at such close quarters that you have a chance to seize your opponent or his weapon, remember that a swiftly delivered Jiu-jitsu kick or blow is a much quicker way to get him. Keep at him and throw him off his balance as taught you in the classes, and this will result in bringing him to the ground much more quickly than if you attempted to grasp him or his weapon and throw him.

It does not require strength to throw a man off his balance; a slight push on the shoulders is usually quite enough. It is an easily acquired knack once you have grasped the idea that the center of gravity lies in the stahara, two inches below the navel. By practicing the stahara exercises you learn how to retain your own balance.

The trick illustrated by the photo shows a chance that might often occur in the trenches. Your enemy presses on your rifle, you let go with your left hand and bring the heel of your hand beneath his nose, as shown in the cut on the front cover of this pamphlet. Follow this with the knee on the crotch, and this will give you an opening for the butt of your rifle or the bayonet.

The Bare Hand "Gets" Him Here

6-27-31-1000 (1B-9313)

ANNUAL REPORT OF RESERVE OR RETIRED OFFICER
FOR JULY 31, 1932, UNDER PAR. 19, R-20

Name ALLAN C SMITH
(Print)

Grade MAJOR A.G.D. | National Guard Reserve
~~State Reserve List~~
~~Retired List~~

~~Bus.~~ Address Seventh Regiment Armory, 66 St & Park Ave, New York, N.Y.

~~Bus.~~ Telephone Rhinelander 4-0387

Res. Address Army & Navy Club, 30 West 44 St, New York, N.Y.

Res. Telephone Vanderbilt 3-5360

U. S. Reserve Corps status (if any) Rank _____ Branch _____

3-12-32-5000 (1B-5967)

SERVICE RECORD

B-DCN-SCH-ETC.	UNITED STATES		MILITIA	
Smith, Allan C.	WW–Pvt Inf (NA)	12 Jun 18	Capt Inf RI	13 Dec 20
B-Scotland	Capt Inf (NA)	16 Jul 18	Capt AGD SS	19 Sep 21
4 Feb 84	HD	30 Nov 20	Maj	27 Dec 27
			HD	30 Dec 27
			Maj AGD RL	30 Dec 27
			Dtld Actv Duty (NY State Police Sch)	9 Jan 28
			to	16 Feb 28
			HD (81 ML)	1 Dec 38

FULL NAME (LAST NAME FIRST)

SMITH, ALLAN CORSTORPHIN

| A RED | NGR. BLUE | R L GREEN | RETIRES YELLOW |

THE
BATTLE FIGHTING
COMBATIVES OF
ALIAN C. SMITH

INSTRUCTOR TO THE
NEW YORK STATE TROOPERS

In 1922, an article in the **Evening Telegram** on February 5th, states that a Philippine Veteran who knows bone-crushing and paralyzing tricks is preparing a painful surprise for unsuspecting lawbreakers. The article incorrectly claims that Smith learned jiu jitsu while stationed in the Philippines.

"There is a certain military officer who served as a captain in the army while in the Philippines. While there he learned secrets from the natives which are to prove of inestimable value to the State of New York."

The article claims that upon his return from the Philippines, "Captain Smith now and then found it necessary to mildly practice his jiu-jitsu, and it got out that he was the white hope of disarmament advocates. The matter came to the attention of Adjutant General J. Leslie Kincaid, who conceived the idea that were Smith to instruct the members of the National Guard the need for ammunition would be reduced to a minimum and the chances would be better of his appropriations being approved by the financial chairman of an economical administration."

Kincaid "saw to it that Captain Smith was assigned to jiu-jitsu instruction work at division headquarters in New York City, not, however, until he had playfully dug General Kincaid in the ribs, all but tossed him over his head and demonstrated beyond doubt that the power of the human hand, arm and knee might be made as potent as gunshot."

Soon Major George F. Chandler, the Superintendent of the New York State Police heard of Smith and sought out General Kincaid and with the General's approval Chandler made a proposition to Smith to become an instructor at the State Trooper School. Smith agreed.

"Captain Smith is looked upon by Major Chandler as his luckiest find. He says that when his troopers become proficient in jiu-jitsu they will be able to accomplish wonders, and their ability to deal summarily with wrongdoers will be markedly intensified."

An article in **The Times-Union**, on June 26th, 1923 describes Smith giving a lecture to sixty policemen, and he is working alongside Chandler who lectured the recruits on keeping in physical condition. Smith was the first lecturer of the day and he confined the first day's efforts to deportment, neatness and simple military rules of conduct applicable to the police office.

"When you give an order give it in a voice that suggests authority," Smith says, "Now then, heels together, snap." The article states that "the first class in the police school, snapped their heels together, a little awkwardly at first, but after a half hour's practice they could snap nearly as well as the instructor."

In 1925, in the **Troy Times**, Smith who was now a Major sought to try out a system of education and training among school children designed to eliminate the cause and the effects of panics and deaths due to fires in schools and in crowded buildings of all descriptions. He enlisted the aid of the Superintendent of Schools Eldred in trying out the system.

"Wednesday morning of next week the Major will take over two classes as a test of the system, which he describes briefly as "teaching the young to be light on their feet, to keep to the right, and to talk quietly."

Smith says that "At many of the school and theatre disasters many people are trampled on or crushed to death rather than from the actual fire. By teaching them what I call 'Individual alertness' they learn to move quickly and lightly with consideration for the other person, to pass and repass without stumbling or tripping the other fellow, and to have a perfect mental and physical coordination which enables them to think and act quickly at all times."

Smith said that his system would "eliminate panics and a good deal of confusion at the school under the present disciplinary drills, and will also cut in half the number of children killed by automobile accidents."

He goes on to say "With these objects and these promises I have made a trial should show whether or not the system is as successful in

Troy schools as in other places, and I see no reason why the system should not work out as well here, as elsewhere."

True to form Smith was engaged in presenting his views and methods on the subject in book form. The article goes on to state that his duties at the Police School brought him to Troy two days each week, but "I will be willing to donate my services to the city, and to come from New York for four days if the system should be adapted here." Smith would later use elements of this program for the "Castle of Safety" at the World's Fair when he worked as the Commander-in-Chief of the safety monitors.

> **MAJOR ALLAN SMITH**
> of the Knickerbocker Greys will train your boy in Swimming, canoeing, boating, Jujitsu, baseball, shooting, riding, singing, fishing, etc., at Lake George Camp, 700 acres, one mile shore front. Motorboats, trips. Resident Doctor. Christian camp. Write for booklet to
> **MAJOR ALLAN SMITH**
> Dept T,
> 245 Central Park West, New York

Ad in the classified section/camp directory of the New York Tribune, May 4, 1930

An article in **The Attica News** in 1932 has Smith teaching the last four days of a training school course for Prison Guards. Voice training, correct posture and the proper methods of giving commands were the principal subjects of Smith's lecture periods at the prison school.

He declared to the guards and to the press that those subjects are the only ones for good guard work as guards who are equipped with those principals can command the respect of their charges and he considered them of greater importance than the extensive training of jiu jitsu despite the prospects of hand-to-hand combat being far greater for prison guards than in any other police service. The article notes that a prison guard is not permitted to carry a weapon other than a stick.

Smith said, "He must look the prisoner in the eye when he gives a command, must be up-standing and fearless and by his voice, posture and demeanor win the respect of those he is commanding."

Getting into a general discussion of his methods Smith said that the pacifistic opposition to such training was short sighted. Smith said "It is training for peace as much as it is training for war. We do not want to become a military country as Germany did and as Japan is now doing, but the need of fearless, courageous citizens is as great in times of peace as in war times. We may never have war again but there will always be shipwrecks, panics and disaster. What happens when there is a short circuit in the subway in New York City? A panic. People are always injured but you never hear of anyone being burned. The same thing happens when there are fires where there are public gatherings. Training of the eye, the body, and the voice as a national movement for boys would do away with much of this. Smith was again laying the groundwork for what would later be the World's Fair, boy scout safety monitors.

On January 4th, 1937 in an article in **The Poughkeepsie Eagle-News**, Smith promised state troopers attending the 16th annual school that at the end of the months' session they would emerge with streamlined habits of mind and body.

He says "You have observed men from West Point and Annapolis. You know what an alertness and poise they have that seems indefinable. You have envied them. Don't. In one month, I will make you better than any West Pointer."

Smith said he would teach the men "how to disable and even kill an opponent who attacks them when they are unarmed."

"Each man will practice each trick 100 times on someone else and have it practiced a hundred times on himself and there will be no injuries in the school."

One final incident during the interwar years is worth a mention. In **The Gettysburg Times**, March 19th, 1930 there is an article which describes a captain who will defend himself against twelve men. The article states "If you are attacked by an assailant with a rifle, a pistol or a knife, or if some burly husky swoops down upon you, it is not impossible to defend yourself successfully and gain an advantage over your assailant, according to Captain Wilbur R. McReynolds, assistant commandant of the R.O.T.C. unit at Gettysburg college."

To prove his assertion Captain McReynolds demonstrated modern methods of defense against an attack by twelve men, as one of the many features of an indoor circus which was to be staged at the Eddie Plank Memorial gymnasium.

He would demonstrate how to ward off an attack by the twelve men, two of them armed with rifles, two with pistols, two with knives and six using strong arm methods.

According to the article the feat sounds almost impossible but the 155 pound captain had already previously demonstrated how simple it was when one is acquainted with the various means of defense.

Captain McReynolds had been one of thirty army officers selected by the government to take a special course in defense methods and jiu jitsu under Captain Allan Smith at Fort Benning, Georgia. The thirty officers then toured the army cantonments instructing other officers and noncoms.

Captain McReynolds would demonstrate the various methods first in slow motion, explaining the various details, grips, holds and methods of throwing an attacker to the ground or disarming him of a rifle, pistol, knife or any other weapon used by the assailant.

Then the twelve men would attack the captain who would successfully ward off each attack in quick succession. In fast motion the captain would be able to defend himself against the twelve men in less than one minute. Each of them would wear jackets similar to those used by the Japanese, called *Judogi*.

The captain had already achieved considerable success in this field. He had toured the New England states vaudeville circuit with an army platoon, which was especially selected to compete against representatives of the marines and the navy.

According to the article the army team had won the contest and was invited to tour a vaudeville circuit. General Clarence R. Edwards presented Captain McReynolds' outfit with a silver cup which was emblematic of their victory over the navy and marine outfits.

The indoor circus at which Captain McReynolds would stage his exhibition was sponsored by the Rotary and Lions' clubs and the athletic department of the college for the benefit of the boy's work fund.

There is no follow up article describing if Captain McReynolds was successful or not but presumable he was as he had reputable instructor.

JU JITSU
THE JAPANESE ART OF SELF DEFENSE

A limited number of men and women will be accepted for instruction in the art of Ju Jitsu. Knowledge of this art gives both men and women the utmost advantages in self protection. Classes will be conducted at Troy Y. M. C. A. Building by **MAJOR ALLAN SMITH** Recognized teacher of the art. Instructor New York State Police. Classes on Tuesday and Wednesday at 5:15. Enroll by phone, Troy 200, or call in person. FEE FOR THIS COURSE AT A SPECIAL RATE OF $5.00. This extremely low rate is offered to stimulate public interest toward an art of defense in which every man, woman and child should be proficient. Separate classes for men and women.

Advertisement in *The Times Record*, Troy, New York, January 20, 1940

Safety Monitors at the World's Fair

An article in the **Brooklyn Eagle** on November 11th, 1938, written by Eugene Du Bois describes Smith's duties as the Commander-in-Chief of Safety Monitors. Du Bois says that the "New York World's fair, 1939 is resplendent with uniforms but there is no one in Flushing Meadow who wears his with more distinction and military bearing than Major Allan Smith."

Smith was the drillmaster to the Fair's special police and in addition he was the commander-in-chief of the Safety Monitors. The article states that it was the latter that were Smith's pride and joy. They were Boy Scouts selected from the five boroughs for volunteer duty on the grounds.

250 of them had been going to the Fair each Saturday morning for six weeks for a two-hour session to receive instruction in posture, politeness, attention to duty, clear method of giving commands or directions, and the handling of crowds as well as safety and traffic drills. The recruits were reviewed by Grover A. Whalen, the president of the Fair corporation, and awarded their merit badges of office.

Whalen said "The scout work now to be started has been arranged through the generous co-operation of Charles M. Heistand, Director of Training for the Scout Foundation of New York, and the five borough scout executives. It represents a most important step in our effort to make every child 'safety-minded' not only while visiting the Fair but for the future as well. This will not only be a factor in preventing accidents at the Fair, but should tend to make children safety-conscious at all times."

They were then used by Smith to help instruct 2,000 to 3,000 other Scouts who would assist as members of the safety legion. Their chief duties would be in the "Children's World" part of the Fair, where they would take turns manning a "Castle of Safety" where they would demonstrate the virtues of Boy Scoutism and they would act as aides to the regular policemen and guides. They would also be called upon to form Guards of Honor for special occasions and special ceremonies when distinguished guests visited the Fair, such as President Franklin D. Roosevelt who was flanked by an honor guard of 2,000 uniformed Boy Scouts when he arrived at the World's Fair grounds to take part in the dedication of the Federal Building.

The "Castle of Safety" contained exhibits illustrating the prevention of accidents in the street and in the home, and members of the Legion and their monitors would conduct "tests" for the benefit of visiting youngsters to see if they would look to the left and to the right for traffic and walk lightly on their toes and restrain themselves from screaming when excited.

Du Bois writes that "The interest of his young recruits is held by Major Smith through his own fascinating personality and the bonnie Scotch accent with which he issues his commands. He tells the boys that they are getting essentially the same drill as he gives the New York State Police in their annual training."

Du Bois goes on to state that "Smith has drilled the State Police, the Knickerbocker Grays and innumerable boys in schools and Summer camps. He acted as a consultant to various principals and headmasters faced with refractory and disobedient pupils, and is frequently called in to make boys behave when their teachers let them get out of hand."

Smith is "able to do this because he has a keen understanding of human nature and the likes and dislikes of the average boy. The bad habits of the young, says he, fall into nine major categories, all correctable."

Du Bois says that Smith is firm but never harsh in dealing with the youngsters. He appeals to them through similies such as "Be light-toed like an Indian," or "Be quiet in your chairs like cavalry officers on horseback," or "Be polite to strangers like a State Trooper."

Smith's method brought results and it was for that reason that the Boy Scouts flocked to take his instruction at the Fair. "He has succeeded there in making the boys get as much fun in preparing for safety as boys in Europe do in preparing for war. He calls his instructions the "West Point of Safety," and he makes the boys take their anti-shoving, anti-screaming, anti-stumbling and anti-panic drills in preparation for the World's Fair just as seriously as if they were doing anti-air raid and anti-gas drills in London at the time of the recent international crisis."

The Safety Monitor Cadets which was founded at the World Fair morphed into an organization called the Emergency Service Cadet Corps or the Queens Military Brigade which consisted of about 30 members. In the Long Island Daily Press, on Saturday, May 8th, 1942, 17-year-old, City College student, Morton Raymond, one of the scouts who had been chosen by Smith for the Safety Monitor Cadets, became one of the highest ranking commissioned officers in the Cadet Corps. About his time in the Safety Monitor Cadets he explains "We were taught how to handle crowds and how to handle ourselves in an emergency situation."

All of the 30 members of the corps had completed the standard Red Cross first aid course and many of them had gone on to complete the advanced course as well. The members of the Brigade in South Queens volunteered their services as messengers for the Air Raid Protection Service.

Regarding Smith who was the team chairman Raymond says "Last February, Major Smith was called from the Army Reserve into active duty. He is now a captain in the military police. Before he went into active service he appointed Major John Crane of Jamaica as our adult supervisor. We have been carrying on by ourselves and now feel that we are ready to start a membership drive so that we can teach safety and first aid to other boys and girls." Smith had also been working as the Executive Director for the Red Cross, Central Queens Chapter prior to being called into active duty.

JIU-JITSU CLASS IN ACTION
Captain Raymond, at left, points out the technique.

The corps met every Saturday at the Lost Battalion Hall in Elmhurst, Queens. The two-hour drill sessions taught the cadets how to move swiftly and carefully in large groups. The article states that the knowledge would be of inestimable value if it were necessary to evacuate children from schools, theaters, churches or other public places.

In addition to the safety drills which were taught, the boys were given fencing and rifle instruction. Major Crane was the rifle and fencing instructor. About the corps Raymond said "We want to get new members. We offer instruction in military training, first aid, fencing and rifle. The boys over 16 will find this knowledge helpful. If an emergency situation comes up here in Queens, everyone with a knowledge of first aid will be a valuable citizen in the community."

He continues "The younger children will benefit by the safety training we can give them. It will teach them to be careful in their daily lives and to some extent, it will teach them to be self-reliant. That knowledge will also be important if an air raid comes to Queens.

"If trained youngsters will be able to get to a place of safety without getting in the way of adults, it is plain that we will have accomplished something. We hope to build a large organization because we honestly believe that we have something valuable to offer to those who wish to become members of our group."

It had been planned that boxing and jiu-jitsu classes would be instituted before Major Smith was called to active service. The article states that Smith was pleased by the enthusiasm which the boys showed for the sport. Unfortunately for them, with Smith being called into active duty plans for those courses were dropped temporarily.

WORKING FOR THE RED CROSS

Smith seemed to be the type of person who could not take a day's rest. While residing at the New York University Club located at 4 West 43rd Street and while he was training the Queens Military Brigade, prior to being called to active duty Smith had been elected as the executive director of the Central Queens Red Cross chapter, in July 1940.

During his time working as executive director the Red Cross was involved in sending packages of food to prisoners of war in Europe, making garments for war relief victims, running blood drives, and teaching free courses in First Aid, Water Safety, Accident Prevention and Home Hygiene.

In one newspaper article Smith said "The American Red Cross has always been the leading organization for alleviating suffering in times of disaster. We face a possible disaster. The American Red Cross plays an important part in the National Defense Program. Our citizens must be trained as well as our soldiers and sailors. As part of this National Defense Program, as many citizens as possible should be educated in First Aid and Home Hygiene."

For the Fourth of July weekend that year Smith laid down seven precautionary rules advocated by the chapter's First Aid, Water Safety and Accident Prevention Bureaus. Rules that still pertinent in today's world.

The rules for motorists were:
- Check the tires, brakes, steering and lights on your car now.
- Beat traffic congestion by starting early.
- Don't pile luggage so high it obscures side or rear vision.
- Sacrifice that last hour at the beach or picnic and leave before the crowd.
- Slow up when the sun goes down—night driving is hazardous.

The rules for bathers:
- Swim only at patrolled beaches.
- Don't swim too soon after eating.

At one point American Red Cross contributors had to be reassured by Smith that the war relief to the conquered countries of Europe would not prolong hostilities by providing indirect assistance to Germany. In August of 1940, Smith had to make a statement addressing those concerns in the Long Island Star Journal.

In the article titled Unfounded Rumor Hinders Urgent Work, Smith writes "On Monday, Nov. 11, the annual Red Cross Roll Call started. On that day hundreds of thousands of volunteer workers have a great task before them. It is their duty to ask everyone to join the Red Cross, that its work may be continued throughout the world at a time when the world needs humanitarianism more than ever before. It is important then, that everyone understand the clear purpose of the Red Cross so that he will know why he is being asked to give.

"It has come to our attention that rumors are being circulated which may tend to hamper the work by raising doubt as to the worthiness of the Red Cross cause.

"These rumors are in no way based on fact. For the most part they are circulated unthinkingly and with a fine disregard for the harm they might eventually do.

"Since the war began, the bulk of Red Cross work has been concentrated in Europe, bringing aid to wounded soldiers and to civilians. Early this summer when France fell, any persons feared that Red Cross funds and materials would be commandeered by the German army to be used in furthering their war against the Allies. Rumors to this effect have persisted.

"The answer to these rumors is: Not a single garment has gone to the European continent since July; not even the unoccupied area of France is getting Red Cross aid today.

"It is important to estimate the harm these rumors have already done in preventing citizens from helping. We feel the time has come when these malicious falsehoods should end. We are therefore calling on each of you to stop this effort to block the work of humanitarianism."

Smith then goes on to say how much has been contributed and says the fundraising drive "is progressing satisfactorily, notwithstanding the circulation of false rumors. But I should like to leave with you the thought that it is impossible to give too much to the Red Cross. That old slogan of World War days still holds good: GIVE UNTIL IT HURTS!"

Smith seemed to have had much success while working for the Red Cross but once he was called back to service it seemed that his focus had shifted back to instructing jiujitsu and teaching things that were less humanitarian in nature..

And Every Hand Was for the Red Cross

With war in Europe making terrific demands on the American Red Cross, the organization needs all the help it can get, so the St. Albans Auxiliary extended a helping hand—in fact, many helping hands—at a card party in the American Legion Hall, 194-15 Linden boulevard, St. Albans. Shown participating in one of the games are, left to right, Irene Leminsky, Major Allan Smith, executive director of the Central Chapter of Queens; Ella V. Rhoads, general chairman of the party, and Adele Keller, auxiliary chairman.

Give Him The Once Over

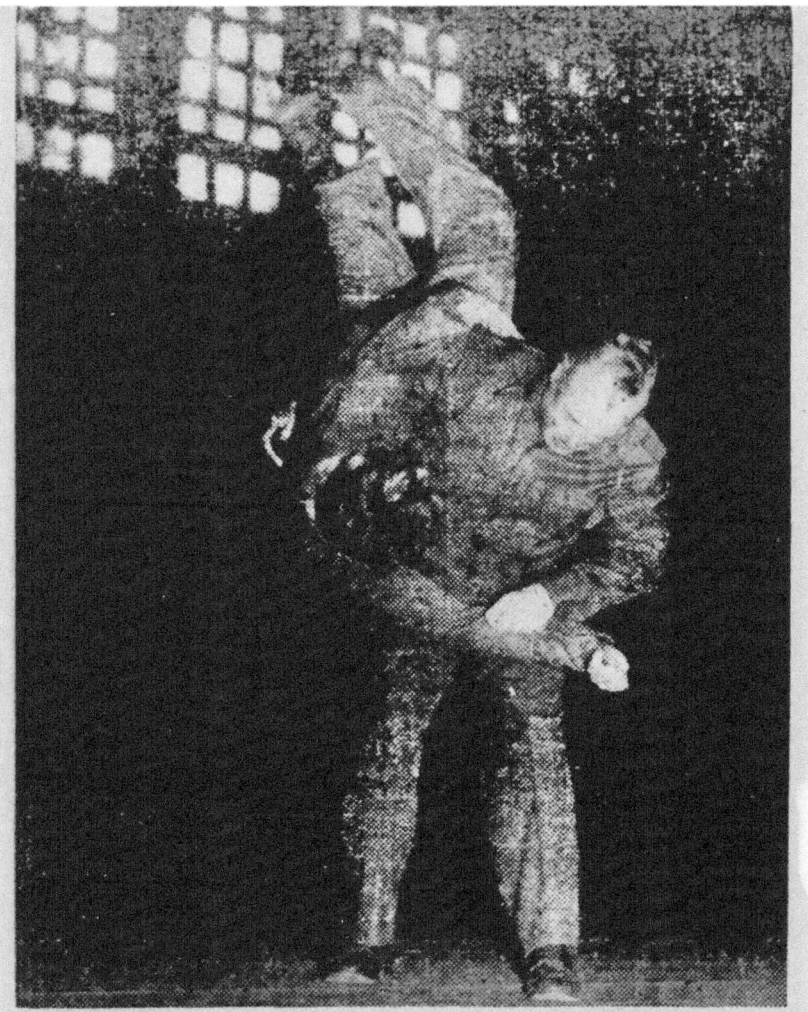

Here's Capt. Allen C. Smith, top judo instructor, demonstrating that life in the army is sometimes very upsetting. Capt. Smith has been giving officers of the 13th armored a few gentle hints on how to influence and eliminate people.

THE

BATTLE FIGHTING

COMBATIVES OF

ALLAN C. SMITH

BATTLE-FIGHTING

In 1943 Smith was again back to his old ways, teaching troops the art of killing a man with their bare hands and feet. He was teaching a class of 80 officers of the 13th armored division his course was officially called "hand-to-hand Combat" but later articles stated that he termed his course "**Battle Fighting**." When the pupils completed the course they would in turn go back to their outfits to instruct their men in the methods of dirty fighting.

In the **Appeal Democrat**, Wednesday, March 31st Smith said "Whenever the American public hears Judo mentioned, they visualize the various grips and muscular releases that policemen use in disarming law breakers. These methods are effective in their proper place, but are far too complicated."

In a return to his old days when he started training troops with his six lessons in 1917, Smith now taught three basic type of attacks, which could be learned quickly. He emphasized proper mental attitude and alertness.

It's interesting to note that perhaps because of the attitudes of the time period toward the Japanese, it was no longer mentioned in the articles that the driving force of his system was Stahara. Perhaps it was a personal choice on Smith's part not to mention something even remotely Japanese sounding as Stahara in the articles, and instead he called his system something much more in keeping with the times, he called his system, Battle Fighting.

For training purposes certain holds were barred, but Smith made sure his students would know how to make full use of them when the time came for some cold-blooded killing.

Despite the strenuousness of the training, there had been no serious injuries in any of the many classes he taught.

Smith made it clear much as he did in the 1918 pamphlet that sportsmanship had to be confined to the classes – with the enemy they had to fight dirty. In the March 24th 1943 issue of the **Appeal Democra**t, Smith says "American fair play in sports or war is idealistic but it doesn't fit this war, and if you would survive be prepared to use even dirtier tactics than the enemy can imagine."

In an article in the **Star Tribune** on June 10th, the 59-year old Smith describes his system of Battle Fighting. He writes,

"Give a battalion of men three months training in Judo and then put them up against a battalion of my men trained for a week in battle fighting. I'll guarantee every one of them will be dead in 30 seconds."

He went on to explain that Battle fighting is an exposition of the three Ms—*Mayhem, Maiming,* and *Mutilation.*

"In battle" he argued, "you have neither the time nor opportunity to use fancy holds. That's what Judo is. As a matter of fact, Judo is just an adaptation of ju-jitsu as taught to police and other civilians."

He goes on to say that "Battle fighting emphasizes quick footwork, crippling kicks in the groin, and either a front or rear strangle-hold to crush a man's Adam's apple."

Much like his time training in the various camps during World War 1, Smith was traveling through several Southern camps where he was expounding his hand-to-hand combat tactics. At the time of the article he had been stationed at Camp Hood, Texas for six months.

Smith called his job "the most hazardous in the army." Explaining that enthusiastic pupils were always trying to land a killing blow against him.

As a diversion he sent unit after unit in what he described as "battle wrestling" a nicer version of battle fighting in which kicking, gouging and biting were barred.

Smith said "It's more realistic than boxing and better physical training. You line 'em up, one behind another, in opposing teams. The leaders go at it, and one or the other usually is defeated in 30 seconds. The winner takes on the next man, and so on, usually until he, himself. Is beaten. Then the man behind him steps up. Thus the strongest may be defeated, and the weakest is always striving to wear down a stronger opponent so he will be defeated by the man behind. It's the toughest sport in the world."

On January 14th, 1946, in an article in the Daily Boston Globe, Alan Smith the 60 year old veteran is mentioned as the head instructor, along with about 14 war veterans all of whom saw overseas action, at a training school for officers and instructors who were heading to Palestine to join the Jewish liberation movement. The head of this school was Aron Z. Propes who was described as a former Latvian Army officer.

FUTURE FIGHTERS—With keen interest a class of 'teen-age Jews follows a demonstration by former Maj. Allen Smith.

The article states that more than 100 young men and women, including World War II veterans were in training so far. The course of training at the "Zionist Officer's Training School," was conducted twice a week for three months, in a Harlem gymnasium. It is here that the trail for Smith runs cold.

Maj. Allen Smith, instructor, and members of his jiu-jitsu class watching Evelyn Antonoff throw Marvin Lieberman to the floor with a hip lift.

I was able to find a legal notice in the **Long Island Star-Journal**, in 1963 regarding an Allan C. Smith who at the time of his death was a resident of 147-38 Barclay Avenue, in Flushing, Queens but I was unable to confirm that it is the same Allan C. Smith. To my knowledge, Smith never married or had any children so the person mentioned in the notice very well could have been him; however I would prefer not to think of the end of his life this way, that he died in obscurity.

For someone who gave so much of his time furthering various noble causes, it's hard to stomach that the Stahara Kid had died and there was no obituary for him at the end of his life; only a legal notice for creditors to come forward. He accomplished a lot in his lifetime and should be recognized for his accomplishments. Hopefully my research here has remedied that somewhat.

END COMMENTS

When I set out to conduct research for writing this book, my goal was to give exposure to some of the unknown instructors of hand-to-hand combat training in the United States during both of the World Wars. We often approach the Combatives discipline today from the perspective that it was Fairbairn who was largely responsible for propagating this type of training in the United States. If one were to focus solely on Fairbairn, Applegate, and Biddle then they would not be acknowledging the work and time put in by many of the other patriotic people who stepped forward to do their part. People like Allan Smith.

All of these people provided the troops with the knowledge that they would be able to handle themselves in a situation where they had to resort to hand-to-hand fighting. It is possible that the soldiers or spies who were taught the techniques never used any of it; however, there were other benefits in learning these techniques such as a feeling of confidence that comes from knowing such techniques.

In an April 5th, 1945 memo written by William J. Donovan, the Director of the Office of Strategic Services, with the subject being Recommendation for the Award of the Legion of Merit for Lt. Col. William E. Fairbairn, Donovan writes:

> "In initiating training in close contact fighting, 'gutter' methods in offensive and defensive tactics were taught to the personnel assigned for such training. This was essential to overcoming the natural reluctance and aversion of the typical American soldier (and the British

soldier) to unfair and unethical methods of fighting in which acts of artifice, force, vehemence and shock are of major importance and in which all earmarks of the concepts of fair play and good sportsmanship must be eliminated.

"With the building up of natural confidence in the ability of each man to perform duties of this nature, their training began to show results and their efficiency continuously increased. From reports from overseas theaters, it has been noted that irrespective of whether or not personnel who have undergone this type of training make use of it in the missions to which they are assigned, the mere fact that they have been so trained and have been imbued with the confidence which comes from it, their efficiency in other types of combat operations, and their morale, is greatly increased."

Essentially, Smith was stating the same thing when he discussed his Battle-Fighting Program. I plan on furthering my research regarding several other individuals who taught these type of hand-to-hand combat programs during the First and Second World Wars; individuals who had similar backgrounds as Fairbairn but may not have received as much exposure. Some of them may have even had no desire to have such exposure. They did their patriotic duty and did not expect anything in return.

Several had boxing, wrestling or martial arts backgrounds and were qualified to handle this type of training and instruction; people such as Arvin Ghazlo and Ed Don George. It is my opinion that these individuals deserve some acknowledgment and exposure as well. Some did in their day but have since been forgotten to time. I feel that it is necessary to shine the light on their achievements again. They made a difference.

About the Editor

Mr. Sabet has been interested in the Martial Arts since he was a young boy growing up as an expat in Thailand. He was always interested in History and loved to hear all the stories that the old-timers had to tell. As a teenager, he got into Rock music and started one of the first Punk bands in Thailand with his friends. When he went off to College in Washington State, he stuck to his interests, taking lessons in Judo and playing in loud bands. After College and having worked a few dead end jobs, he decided it was time to move to NYC to be closer to family, where he experienced all that the city had to offer, including the horrific 9/11 attacks. As the years went by he continued to dabble in different martial arts and to research various stories, most of which were local interest related.

One such story that has taken him several years to research and write, is a True Crime story about a bank robbery which occurred in the 1950s. Through the course of his study, he discovered that some of the criminals involved had been Veterans of the 2nd World War. This discovery led him to delve deeper into what particular skill-set a veteran might have and utilize for good or bad after returning from a War.

It was during this process of discovery that Mr. Sabet had arrived at the knowledge of WW II-Era Hand to Hand Combat.

BIBLIOGRAPHY

Bowen, Richard. Some **Background on Captain Allan Corstorphin Smith,** *Author Of Secrets Of Jiu-jitsu: A Complete Course In Self Defense.* Journal Of Non-lethal Combatives, June 2003

Batchelder, Roger. **Camp Upton** *Described and Photographed by the Author.* 1918

Corstorphin Smith, Allan. **10 Ways To "Get" A Boche.** Unpublished, 1918

— **The Secrets of Jiu-jitsu**, *A Complete Course In Self Defense.*

Drexel-Biddle,(Col.) A. J. **Do or Die**, *A Manual on Individual Combat.* 1937

Fairbairn, (Capt.) William E. **All-In-Fighting**. London and New York: D. Appleton Co. 1942

Hancock H., and Katsukuma Higashi. **Complete Kano Jiu-Jitsu** (Judo) by, 1905

Raycroft, Joseph E **Mass Physical Training** for Use in the Army and the Reserve Officer's Training Corps. Washington, DC: Government Printing Office. 1920

Made in the USA
Coppell, TX
13 October 2024